JOSEPH GLANVILL

SCEPSIS SCIENTIFICA
OR
THE VANITY OF DOGMATIZING

Elibron Classics
www.elibron.com

OR,

CONFEST *IGNORANCE*,

THE WAY TO *SCIENCE*;

IN AN *ESSAY* OF THE

VANITY OF DOGMATIZING,

AND

CONFIDENT OPINION.

EDITED, WITH INTRODUCTORY ESSAY,

BY

JOHN OWEN.

KEGAN PAUL, TRENCH & CO

AN ESSAY

ON

THE LIFE AND WORKS OF JOSEPH GLANVILL.

AN ESSAY

ON

THE LIFE AND WORKS OF JOSEPH GLANVILL.

OF the great and many-sided mental throes through which England passed in the 17th century, especially of the reaction, political, religious, and literary, which is marked by the Restoration, it would be hard to find a better exponent than the author of the *Scepsis Scientifica*. Glanvill's was one of those eclectic, sympathetic intellects, which, like a glass with many facets, reveals in brilliant prismatic hues not one or two, but all the great Thought-forces which surround it ; while in response to this varied intellectual sensitiveness, doubtless serving also as a stimulus, was his environment ; for his lot chanced to be cast in one of the most stirring epochs of English History.

The chief events in Glanvill's uneventful life may be briefly summarized. He was born at Plymouth, in 1636. Of his earlier life and education we have no trustworthy record beyond a few casual hints scattered throughout his writings.* He seems to have been brought up, if not as an extreme sectary, at least in some school of Puritanism which allowed small scope for independent judgment. Thus he tells us, in his "*Plus Ultra*" (p. 142): "In my first education I was continually instructed into a religious and fast adherence to everything I was taught, and a dread of disputing in the least article,"—a mode of education which he was wont in after life vehemently to denounce. He entered the University of Oxford in 1652, and took his degree three years after. In the dearth of more direct information, his love of culture and mental independence may fairly be inferred from his associates. Thus he was a personal friend of, and for some few years chaplain to, the well-known Francis Rous, Provost of Eton, who, notwithstanding his Puritan proclivities,

* The chief authorities for Glanvill's life—all of them unsatisfactory—are Prince's *Worthies of Devon*, p. 431, the *Biographia Brittanica, ad. voc.*, and Horneck's Preface to Glanvill's Remains.

and the facility with which he accommodated himself to Cromwell's designs, was a man of considerable culture as well as liberality. Another of his theological friends was Baxter,* while his circle of literary and scientific acquaintance comprised names as famous as Boyle and Meric Casaubon. Glanvill used to lament in after life that his friends had not sent him to Cambridge, so that he might have reached the "New Philosophy" of Descartes—already domiciled in that University—by a shorter route than that which his circumstances compelled him to follow. Indeed, the Aristotelianism which was still the ruling philosophy of Oxford seems to have sat as heavily on Glanvill's soul as did the Puritan dogmatism which was its prevailing type of religion. From these twin Incubi he resolved to free himself at the earliest possible moment. His liberation from Aristotle is marked by the publication of his first work, in 1661, while the Restoration may be taken as the date of his emancipation from the religious thraldom of Puritanism. No sooner had that

* Comp. *Reliquiæ Baxterianæ*, Pt. ii. p. 378.

b

event taken place, than Glanvill renounced the small modicum of Nonconformity he had hitherto professed, and took orders in the Church of England. Of this conduct Anthony Wood characteristically remarks, that at the Restoration "Glanvill turned about and became a Latitudinarian," but the altered position thus sneeringly alluded to was in Glanvill's case, as in that of others, not so much a change of front as a natural and inevitable movement in advance. His own judgment of such a transformation by development is indicated in his account of Bishop Rust, who similarly took advantage of the Restoration to "turn about" from Puritanism to the English Church. "He was one of the first," says Glanvill, "that overcame the prejudices of the education of he late unhappy times in that University (Cambridge), and was very instrumental to enlarge others. He had too great a soul for the trifles of that age, and saw early the nakedness of phrases and phancies. He outgrew the pretended orthodoxy of those days, and addicted himself to the Primitive Learning and Theology, in which he even then became a great master." Glanvill soon became a marked man among the clergy of his time, and his preferment was rapid. First instituted to a small rectory in Essex, he was promoted shortly after to the vicarage of Frome, in Somerset. About the same date (1664) he was made a fellow of the newly-founded Royal Society—an honour which he seems to have attained by his attack on Aristotle and Scholasticism, and his enlightened advocacy of the new methods of Descartes and Bacon. In 1666 he became Rector of the Abbey Church in Bath, and resided in that city until his death. In 1672 he exchanged the vicarage of Frome for the rectory of Street in Somerset, and about the same time was appointed one of the chaplains in ordinary to Charles II. A few years later (1678) he was installed Prebendary of Worcester. He died of fever in 1680, and was buried in the north aisle of the Abbey Church in Bath, where an inscription may still be seen recording his virtues, and insisting especially on the fact that the twenty-four years of his brief maturity were spent "*in studio et contemplatione verbi et operum Dei.*"

Such are the chronological dry bones of Glanvill's life, and to these, so far as is known, nothing worthy of record can be added. The real extent of his fame and influence must not, however, be meted by the brevity and comparative unimportance of the chief events of his life—the meagreness of his biographical data being largely compensated by the fulness of his literary remains. By his written works, now consigned to, in most instances, a most undeserved oblivion, Glanvill exercised no inconsiderable sway on English thought during the latter half of the 17th century. To the student of that period they still attest his high mental qualities, his keen intellectual perception, his variedly-sensitive imagination, what Wood terms his "quick, warm, spruce and gay fancy," his genial, many-sided receptivity, his fearlessness in enouncing his opinions, his quaint, pithy, pregnant and forcible style. Nor are they of less importance as reflecting the under currents of speculation then in activity among cultured Englishmen. Employing them for this latter purpose, and thereby illustrating the drift of the following treatise, we may take Glanvill as a fair exponent of the following thought-movements of his time. Thus he exemplifies :

1. The Reaction against Philosophical and

Religious Dogmatism, which, though not caused, was materially aided by the collapse of the Puritan *régime.*

2. The study and advocacy of the foreign humanism imported into English literature in the 16th century, but the development of which had been arrested by the rapid growth of Puritanism and by the political troubles of the reigns of James I. and Charles I.

3. The liberalizing tendencies of English Theology, which centred around the school of Divines known as the Cambridge Platonists.

4. The early growth of experimental and natural Science, denoted by Bacon's works and the founding of the Royal Society.

5. The imperfect conception of the true methods of scientific enquiry, which allowed the grossest superstitions a place side by side with the most enlightened researches of Science.

i. Glanvill was one of the first thinkers of the Restoration epoch to place on a philosophical basis the many-sided reaction which forms its chiefest characteristic. Just as Milton recognised an intensified ecclesiasticism in certain forms of Puritanism, Presbyter being but Priest "writ large," so Glanvill and others had no difficulty in detecting beneath its sour austerity and theoretical self-abasement a very real substratum of Omniscience. This was none the less specious in itself or less mischievous in operation for being ostensibly founded on religious sanctions, and assuming the place and function of a divine Revelation. From this standpoint of superior and superhuman knowledge, Puritanism opposed itself to liberal culture of all kinds. Its leaders, excepting a very few far-seeing thinkers, lumped all secular learning under the opprobrious title of "carnal knowledge." Their omniscience rendered all ordinary science superfluous, and the supposedly divine origin of their own enlightenment imparted to every other culture a kind of sinful character. Under these circumstances it was clearly necessary for liberal thinkers like Glanvill to enter the court of human judgment with the counter-plea of Ignorance. The attempt was in its essence precisely that which Sokrates set himself in ancient Greece, and which the leaders of the Renaissance undertook when they opposed the dogmatism of mediæval Rome. In fact, Glanvill and his fellow-thinkers were the apostles of the reactionary doubt which is invariably engendered by excessive or tyrannical dogma. The enterprise was not, however, exclusively secular in their case. The religious dogmatism which they opposed was only part of a general intellectual despotism, under which English thought of the freer sort had long groaned. Aristotle shared with Calvin supreme authority in English opinion- his rule in the realms of science being as absolute as Calvin's in the domain of religious doctrine. There was indeed no little similarity in spirit and method between the two systems, as then conceived and administered ; both agreed, *e.g.*, in arrogating finality each in its own province, and therefore in opposing Novelty of Thought as the deadliest of human errors. According to Bacon's definition, Aristotle was Antichrist, and Glanvill, together with other free-thinkers, were not far wrong in discerning a similar antagonism to Truth in certain phases of Calvinism.

Against these twin giants, the " Pope and Pagan " of English Thought during the first half of the 17th century, Glanvill soon proceeded to set the battle in array. He attacked both the religious and scientific

Dogmatism directly by pointing out their defects, and indirectly by inculcating as a counteracting principle what he terms the sceptical or free Philosophy. His first onslaught was made by his publication, in 1661, of a work entitled "*The Vanity of Dogmatizing or Confidence in Opinions*"— "A remarkable work," says Hallam, "but one so scarce as to be hardly known at all except by name." He republished this work in an altered and improved form in 1665, prefixing to it a warm panegyric on the Royal Society. This amended edition is even rarer than the "*Vanity of Dogmatizing*," the greater part of the impression having been destroyed in the Great Fire. Glanvill entitled it "*Scepsis Scientifica*," and it is this work which is presented to the English reader, after a lapse of two hundred and twenty years, in the ensuing pages.

But although he styled his thought *sceptical*, and himself a *sceptic*, Glanvill did not employ those terms in the commonly received sense of wanton or unreasonable disbelief, but in the classical meaning of enquiry and judicial suspense. It is true he is not careful to discriminate accurately between suspense and negation, and his

definition of *scepsis* is always in the most
general terms,* but there is no mistaking his
usual conception of the principle or the mode
of its application. It is best described as the
principle opposed to excessive dogma,
whether in Philosophy, Science or Religion.
He defends his method in a noteworthy
passage in the second of his collected essays
(p. 44), which, as giving the key-note of the
following treatise, deserves quotation.

* Some mode of discrimination between
Skepticism in its proper and primary sense
of Enquiry, and in its perverted but usual
sense of disbelief or Negation, seems urgently needed. The writer has endeavoured
to effect this in his work, "*Evenings with
the Skeptics,*" and elsewhere, by spelling the
word when employed in its original sense as
Skepticism. The persistent confusion that
occurs between Suspense and Negation,
even in accredited works on Philosophy, is
not very complimentary to the progress of
human thought. Few persons seem able to
realize that *Skepsis* is as much opposed to
Dogmatic Negation as to Dogmatic Affirmation. In pp. 192-3 of the following
treatise the reader will find Glanvill's view of
the relation between Suspense and Negation ; and perhaps the writer may be par-
doned for referring on the same point to his
work on the Skeptics above-mentioned.

" But the True Philosophers are by others accounted *Scepticks* from their way of Enquiry : which is not to continue still poring upon the writings and opinions of Philosophers, but to seek Truth in the great Book of Nature, and in that search to proceed with wariness and circumspection without too much forwardness in establishing maxims and positive doctrines : To propose their opinions as Hypotheseis that may probably be the true accounts, without peremptorily affirming that they are. This among others hath been the way of those great men, the Lord Bacon and Descartes, and is now the method of the Royal Society of London, whose motto is *Nullius in Verba.* This is Scepticism with some, and if it be so indeed, 'tis such Scepticism as is the only way to sure and grounded knowledge, to which confidence in uncertain opinions is the most fatal enemy."

That the mode of thought thus indicated was well adapted to the needs of the time is obvious, though Glanvill never loses sight of the fact that it is likely to operate only among comprehensive and cultured thinkers. Readers of the *Scepsis* will find in chaps. xxvi. and xxvii. remarks on the mischief which he considered had been caused in England by excessive dogma, and similar reflections occur throughout his works. In his defence of the *Scepsis*, *e.g.* he thus addresses his chief antagonist (Thomas White), who was a rabid Aristotelian: "If we differ, then, 'tis only in this, that you think it more suitable to the requisites of the present age to depress scepticism, and perhaps I look on dogmatizing and confident belief as the more dangerous and common evil." But although Glanvill designed his treatise as a counteractive to the thought-tendencies of his time, it is in itself an indirect outcome of the very influences which he deprecates. His assault on the Aristotelian Philosophy is conceived in the spirit and carried out by the method that marks mediæval and scholastic Peripateticism, while he attacks current dogmatic Theology from the basis of the primary article in its creed. The latter point seems to merit a few remarks, as indicating the germ and evolution of his Skepticism. Curious as it may seem, it was a direct outgrowth of his Puritan education, for it had as its starting point, The Fallible nature of humanity by means of the Fall. Few things indeed are more remarkable among the many strange mutual relations of Philosophy and Theology than the reciprocal action of the Philosophical doctrine of the weakness of human reason, and the Theological Dogma of the natural degeneracy of mankind. While among the Greeks and ancient Hindus the experience of intellectual impotence and limitation induced a theory of natural fallibility, among Christian thinkers such as Augustine and Pascal the dogma of the fall issued into a Skeptical theory of Intellectual imperfection. Thus Skepticism is oftentimes found to be in Christian speculation nothing else than the philosophical form of Original Sin. In Glanvill's case the Theological form of the doctrine not only leads up to its philosophical form, but becomes merged and lost in it. He enlarges on this theme more in his *Vanity of Dogmatizing* than in his later *Scepsis Scientifica.* His introductory chapter in the former work consists of some bold speculations as to the perfection of Adam's Intellect before the Fall. So we are told that " all the powers and faculties of this copy of the Divinity, this meddal of God, were as perfect as beauty and harmony in Idea. The soul was not clogg'd by the inactivity of its masse as ours ; nor hindered in its actings by the distemperature of indisposed organs. Passions kept their place as servants of the higher powers, and durst not arrogate the throne as now. . . . . Even the senses, the soul's windows, were without any spot or opacity : to liken them to the purest crystal were to debase them by the comparison . . . Adam needed no spectacles. The acuteness of his natural opticks (if conjecture may have credit) shewed him much of the celestial magnificence and bravery without a Galileo's tube : and 'tis most probable that his naked eyes could reach near as much of the upper world as we with all the advantages of Art . . . . His sight could inform him whether the Loadstone doth attract by Atomical Effluviums . . . . It may be he saw the motion of the blood and spirits through the transparent skin as we do the workings of those little industrious animals (bees) through a hive of glasse. . . . Sympathies and An- tipathies were to him no occult qualities, &c." (*Vanity of Dogmatizing*, pp. 5-7). Much of this introduction may justify Hallam's criticism of it as rhapsodical, and Glanvill's fanciful surmises, which are, however, not more extravagant than similar theological speculations of a bygone age, are considerably toned down in the "*Scepsis*," where the reader will find the following disclaimer, better becoming a Skeptic :—"But a particular knowledge of the blest advantages and happy circumstances of our primitive condition is lost with Innocence, and there are scarce any hints of conjecture from the present." Nevertheless, though more briefly and cautiously, the *Scepsis Scientifica* also insists upon man's inherent incapacity for knowledge, which Glanvill somewhat incongruously both laments as a lapse from his original perfection, and claims as a primary condition of wisdom. The second chapter is on "Our Decay and Ruines by the Fall," and consists of a lengthy elaboration of that subject. Succeeding chapters expand and illustrate the argument of human impotence, and insist on its only possible outcome of scepticism or judicial suspense on most moot points of speculation.

ii. But although the *Scepsis* has its germ in Theological Dogma, its final development in Glanvill's mind must be ascribed to other influences, viz., to the free-thinking liberalizing culture which English literature of the 16th and 17th centuries had derived from Continental sources, chiefly from the leading thinkers of the Italian and French Renaissance. It is not sufficiently borne in mind that the Restoration, which brought back Charles II. and reinstated in a modified form the old monarchy, was also a Restoration of a literary movement which the civil troubles and rapid growth of Puritanism had arrested. During the Elizabethan era the works which still hold their place as the highest products of English culture were indebted largely for suggestion and shaping to Ariosto, Boccaccio, Dante, Montaigne, and Rabelais, and other names of "light and leading" in France and Italy; but during the Civil War and the Commonwealth this importation of foreign thought became almost extinct. The fact, no doubt, admits of easy explanation. These foreign commodities were held to be contraband, for the two reasons that they were incompetent to decide grave questions of political and religious controversy, and their free humanizing tendency was diametrically opposed to the Puritan spirit. They shared the fate which befel all mere secular literature, all culture of the intellect for its own sake. They were sacrificed to that sour disdain of those graces which adorn and refine both letters and human life, which forms the ugliest feature of extreme Puritanism. But the stream of Continental enlightenment from whence Shakespeare and Spencer slaked their thirst had in reality not been destroyed by Puritanism, it had only been dammed, and when it burst its dykes at the Restoration, we cannot be surprised if it displayed all the greater force and volume on account of its confinement. Glanvill's works are among the earliest indications of this reflux of Continental thought. His chief teachers are Descartes, Montaigne, Charron, Gassendi. Many of the utterances in the *Scepsis* would suggest a close study of Montaigne's *Essays.* He often quotes him by name, and never without some commendatory epithet. But it is probable that Glanvill, like Sir Walter Raleigh in his *Sceptick*, may have been indebted largely for his sceptical reasonings either to Henry Stephens' translation of the *Hypotyposes* of Sextus Empeirikos, or to Gassendi's reproduction of the same arguments. In others of his writings Glanvill displays a similar predilection for the leading spirits of what he terms the Free Philosophy. This will serve to account for the suspicion and malevolence which his writings seem to have excited, for he became identified, albeit most unjustly (see his sermon, "Against Scoffing at Religion"), with the excessive libertinism which marked the thought and manners of Charles II.'s reign, and which was largely traceable to Continental sources. Not, however, that these supplied all the motive causes of the reaction. There can be little question that Puritanism, notwithstanding its undeniable merits, helped to engender by its excessive austerity the licence that ensued upon the Restoration. Glanvill fully recognised this fact, and often takes occasion to remark on it in his writings. Thus he observes sententiously in one of his sermons, "The (religious) follies and divisions of one age make way for Atheism in the next." Indeed, Puritanism itself had, as every oppressive scheme of human thought and conduct must needs have, its own licentious side, besides inducing a reactionary excess in other systems. This is abundantly shown by its own distinctive literature, such works, *e.g.* as Edwards' *Gangrena*, and Bailey's *Letters and Journals*. The aim of Glanvill was to direct as far as he could the swollen current of free thought into proper and innocent channels—to show that Continental Humanism and Philosophy were reconcileable with a moderate and rational Christianity; in a word, to prevent intellectual liberty from becoming "a cloke of maliciousness." For such an attempt no commendation can be deemed excessive. The methods of Puritanism, with its extreme other-worldliness, its rigid formalism, its stress on minutiæ in speculation and conduct, its malevolent opposition to every form of recreation and pleasure—whatever appeared likely to enliven human existence —had a peculiarly cramping, numbing influence on men's minds. It operated as Mephistopheles said of the school logic :

"Da wird der Geist euch wohl dressirt
In Spanische stiefeln eingeschnürt."

with the intensification that its strait-lacedness claimed to have a religious basis. Some mode of liberation from this narrow and fanatical obscurantism was urgently needed—what Glanvill indignantly terms "that Barbarism that made Magick of

Mathematics and Heresie of Greek and Hebrew." What his proposed remedy was readers of the *Scepsis* will see for themselves ; but there is one passage in his Essays wherein he speaks so explicitly of the broadening effects of Humanism and the Free Philosophy as opposed to current Superstition, Enthusiasm, and other foes of human Reason and Religion, that it merits quotation. The passage has an additional interest from its relation to Glanvill's well-known opinions on witchcraft. " Superstition consists either in bestowing religious valuation and esteem on things in which there is no good, or fearing those in which there is no hurt. So that this folly expresseth itself one while in doting upon opinions as fundamentals of Faith, and idolizing the little models of fancy for Divine Institutions, and then it runs away afraid of harmless indifferent appointments, and looks pale upon the appearance of any unusual effect of Nature. It tells ominous stories of every meteor of the night, and makes sad interpretations of each unwonted accident. All which are the products of Ignorance and a narrow mind, which defeat the design of Religion, that would make us of a free, manly, and generous spirit, and indeed represent Christianity as if it were a fond, sneaking, weak and peevish thing, that emasculates men's understandings, making them amorous of toys, and keeping them under the servility of childish fears, so that hereby it is exposed to the distrust of larger minds, and to the scorn of Atheists. These and many more are the mischiefs of superstition, as we have sadly seen and felt."

" Now against this evil spirit and its influences the real experimental Philosophy is one of the best securities in the world. For by a generous and open enquiry in the great field of Nature, men's minds are enlarged and taken off from all fond adherencies to their private sentiments. They are taught by it that certainty is not in many things, and that the most valuable knowledge is the practical. By which means they will find themselves disposed to more indifferency towards those petty notions in which they were before apt to place a great deal of religion ; and to reckon that all that will signifie lies in the few certain operative principles of the gospel and a life suitable to such a Faith. . . . Besides which (by making the soul great), this knowledge delivers it from fondness on small circumstances, and imaginary models, and from little scrupulosities about things indifferent, which usually work disquiet in narrow and contracted spirits, and I have known divers whom Philosophy and not disputes, hath cured of this malady." (*Essay* iv., pp. 13-14). In thus asserting a broad culture of Humanism and scientific thought as the best antidote to a narrow, intolerant Theology, Glanvill acted in conformity not only with his own free instincts, but with the best teachings of history—no law of human progress being better attested than the beneficent effects of Nature study and liberal speculation, on those who have been dieted too exclusively on Theological food.

iii. The last sentence of this passage is interesting as probably referring to the Latitudinarians, as they were termed by "men of narrower thoughts and fiercer tempers," says Burnet. They formed that party in the church who found refuge in Philosophical Research and Platonic metaphysics from the religious and other controversies of the time, and whose *credenda* might be succinctly described as Armenianism; A stress upon human Reason as

against extraneous authority ; Aversion to
dogma on speculative subjects ; Belief in
Immutable Morality ; Large if not universal
tolerance of religious opinions ; and Belief
in the Pre-existence of Souls. It is true
Glanvill's name does not occur in ordinary
enumerations of the leaders of this party, or,
if mentioned, occupies only a secondary
place, but readers of the *Scepsis* will readily
perceive how entirely his sympathies accord
with the tenets we have just named. Indeed, with two of the most prominent
members of the party, Dr. Henry More and
Bishop Rust, he seems to have been on
terms of personal and intimate friendship.
It is however certain that he considered
himself as much a member of that school of
thought, as that he was a Fellow of the Royal
Society. Nor does he manifest any dislike
to the epithet Latitudinarian, when duly
interpreted, which was its customary desig-
nation. It conveyed a protest against
narrowness and intolerance, which he appre-
ciated just as heartily as Bishop Thirlwall in
our day, and for the same reason, did the
title of Broad Churchman. Omitting for
lack of space other points of affinity which
connect Glanvill with the Cambridge Pla-

tonists, we limit our remarks to his undogmatic and comprehensive presentation of Christianity, with regard to which he may claim a place second to none of the party.

Glanvill's view of the Christian Religion may be summed up by the epithets Primitive and Rational. Like Pascal he is an example of that appeal to the personal teaching of Christ, which is the best and only resource of the thoughtful intellect, when distracted by conflicting and irrational Dogmas. From the swollen and turbid stream of ecclesiastical tradition, he turns back to the pure and limpid fountain, which rises amid the mountains of Galilee. Hence he assures us that "he owns no opinion in Divinity which cannot plead the prescription of above 1600." . . . . As a believer in Immutable Morality, he contends that, " Divine Truths were most pure in their source and Time could not perfect what Eternity began. Our Divinity, like the Grandfather of Humanity, was born in the fulness of Time, and in the strength of its manly vigour." He maintains a distinction in this respect between Natural and Divine Truth, " Natural Truths are more and more discovered by Time . . . . .

But these Divine Verities are most perfect in their fountain, and original. They contract impurities in their streams and remote derivations." This theme, incidentally touched upon in the "*Scepsis*," is fully developed in his Essays, and in his sermon "On the Antiquity of our Faith" whence the last extract is taken. He calls the two great commandments of the Gospels, "Those Evangelical Unquestionables." The comparative allegiance he conceives himself to own to Primitive Christianity on the one hand, and the tenets of the English Church on the other, he thus indicates :— "Contenting myself with a firm assent to the few Fundamentals of Faith, and having fixed that end of the compass, I desire to preserve my liberty as to the rest, holding the other in such a posture as may be ready to draw these lines, my judgment informed by the Holy Oracles, the Articles of our Church, the apprehensions of wise antiquity and my particular reason shall direct me to describe : and when I do that," he adds with noble and Christian tolerance, "'tis for myself and my own satisfaction. I am not concerned to impose my sentiments upon others, nor do I care to endeavour the change of their minds, though I judge them mistaken, as long as Virtue, the Interests of Religion, the Peace of the World, and their own, are not prejudiced by their errors." Glanvill's significant simile of the compasses, and his idea of the latitude the church allowed in ordinary matters of speculation, receives a further illustration from his preface to " *Lux Orientalis.*" " It is none of the least commendable indulgences of our church that she allows us a latitude of judging in points of speculation, and ties not up men's consciences to an implicit assenting to opinions not necessary or fundamental . . . . Nor is there less reason in this parental indulgence than there is of Christian charity and prudence ; since to tie all others up to our opinions and to impose difficult and disputable matters under the notion of Confessions of Faith, and Fundamentals of Religion, is a most unchristian piece of tyranny, the foundation of persecution, and every root of Antichristianism." Nor is he unprepared with an answer to the delicate and crucial question — What are Fundamentals ? His reply forms the fifth of his Collected Essays, and of a sermon *ad clerum*, which he entitled λογου θρησκεια (The Service of Reason), to which we must refer our readers. Suffice it to say, that Glanvill's opinion of the essentials of Religion is marked by extreme simplicity, the most generous comprehension, and the noblest scorn of long and difficult Creeds and Confessions. Such schemes of Belief were, we need hardly say, very frequent during the years immediately following the Restoration. Hardly a Divine of note could be named, either among the clergy or the Nonconformists, who did not try his hand at devising a system of Belief for the National Church. As a rule these designs serve only to illustrate the narrow conceptions of the would-be ecclesiastical architects. The scheme propounded by Glanvill is probably unique for its exceedingly broad and undogmatic spirit. That it should have been deliberately put forth amid the scenes of ecclesiastical and political tyranny, which disgrace our annals from 1662 onwards, gives it the appearance almost of a grave satirical jest. The church erected on Glanvill's Fundamentals might have been acceptable to some ideal community — some imaginary city of Bensalem, in New Atlantis—it was evidently unsuited by its very excellencies for the England of the 17th century.

iv. But Glanvill is not only an advocate of broad religious and literary culture, as required by the exigencies of his time, he also insists on a specific pursuit of natural science—*i.e.* the New Philosophy of Experiment, such as was taught by Bacon, Descartes and the Royal Society. The advocacy was in truth urgently needed. For we must remember that this new movement of thought, notwithstanding a few propitious circumstances, soon found itself in antagonism to various reactionary forces, which followed upon the Restoration, and which may be described as a recoil towards Mediævalism. It is true the Royal Society received its charter in 1662, and its small band of Fellows were doing their utmost to promote experimental Science as it was then understood ; but this at first was no more than an insignificant back-eddy by the side of a broad and rapid onward current. Of this retrograde movement, the House of Commons, which as Macaulay says, "was more loyal than the King, and more Episcopal than the Bishops," was the political centre, but of its philosophical and Theological phases, the University of Oxford was the stronghold. Here then were two concurrent reactionary movements, each aided by the other, towards Scholasticism in Philosophy, and Sacerdotalism in Theology. The first took the form of an exclusive devotion to Aristotle, and the second so far shared this worship as to maintain that all the Philosophy and Science an orthodox divine needed were contained in the same repository of Greek wisdom. The advice of Marlowe's Faust :—

" Having commenced, be a Divine in show,
   Yet level at the end of every art,
   And live and die in Aristotle's works,"

still summarized the essentials of clerical training as taught by the largest English University. Bearing this in mind, we are able to discern what the animus against Aristotle, disclosed in the *Scepsis Scientifica*, and Glanvill's other writings, really signified. It was not mere opposition to the doctrines of the greatest of Greek Scientific Teachers. From his long and intimate connexion, almost amounting to identification, with mediæval Catholicism, the name of Aristotle had become the symbol of pre-Reformation ideas, not only in Philosophy, but in Theology as well. It was the recognized banner of an antiquated Dogmatism, from which the freer minds of Europe were detaching themselves. The extent of this movement which had derived impetus from the ascendancy of Puritanism (for all the leading Calvinists were Aristotelians) is sufficiently shown by the number of Peripatetic Teachers contemporary with Glanvill, and some of them his own personal antagonists. Even enlightened thinkers, like Meric Casaubon, felt compelled to take up arms in defence of the Stagirite, and to deprecate a too hasty or complete sundering of the associations that clustered round his venerable name. If among a number of concurrent causes, any single one be selected as the chief power, which in England helped to dethrone Aristotle, and the mediævalism with which his name had become identified, it is the foundation of the Royal Society, and the newly awakened enthusiasm, on behalf of Natural Science, of which it was the focus. Those who have dipped into the earlier volumes of the Philosophical

Transactions, are aware of the fact that the proceedings of the Society constituted at first a kind of tacit crusade against Aristotle. No doubt the Society itself was only a practical outcome of the Philosophies of Bacon and Descartes, but it is characteristic of the English intellect, that mere philosophical theory obtains little popular recognition until it has been embodied, enforced and illustrated by actual experiment. Glanvill was a foremost combatant in the struggle. He came forward as the advocate of Freethought and experimental Science, the uncompromising foe of Aristotelianism, the enthusiastic disciple of Bacon and Descartes. To the great French thinker we must ascribe a preponderating share in the moulding of his intellect, for though his veneration for Bacon was great, it was exceeded by his regard for Descartes, whom he addresses in terms of fulsome, and even extravagant, panegyric. He speaks of him as " the grand Secretary of Nature, the miraculous Descartes." " That great man, possibly the greatest that ever was," &c. Probably the more critical analytic and direct method of the French Thinker was better suited to Glanvill's intellect than the practical, yet somewhat ponderous, system of the English Philosopher. Certainly the *Discourse on Method* afforded a shorter road to Skepticism than the devious route supplied by the *Novum Organum.*

Besides the attack on Aristotle contained in the *Scepsis* Glanvill returns to the subject in more than one of his subsequent writings, especially in his work *Plus Ultra,* published in 1668, and afterwards epitomized in the third of his collected *Essays* " Of the modern Improvements of Useful Knowledge." His stand-point in the *Plus Ultra,* and his other writings on the same topic, are even now of considerable interest. We are thereby made aware that Glanvill's age was emphatically an age of Discovery and Invention in every department of human knowledge. Galileo's "tube" was as yet a novelty ; Harvey had not long discovered the circulation of the blood ; the Barometer, Thermometer, Microscope and Air-pump were comparatively recent inventions. New discoveries in Geography, and thereby, as Glanvill remarked, a larger field for human speculation were of continual occurrence. At the very time the *Plus Ultra* was published, Newton, then a young man of

twenty-four, was pursuing those studies
which gave to Glanvill's enthusiastic forecast of the future a far more prophetic
character than he, even in his most sanguine
moments, would have dared to anticipate.
In short, the human intellect, after long
and devious wanderings, had reached the
bounds of the "Wonderland" of Modern
Science, and expectation was rife as to the
disclosures likely to follow ; Glanvill was
one of the first to prognosticate a glorious
future for English and European Science.
His enthusiasm is in part depicted in his
address to the Royal Society, prefixed to
the *Scepsis.* But its fullest expression
is found in his *Plus Ultra.* This is indeed
a cheering cry of "Forward" for all lovers
of Knowledge, as well as a much needed
protest against the Dogmatic and Immobile
"Ne Plus Ultra" of the past.

v. It is with regret that we turn from that
phase of Glanvill's intellect which has most
affinity with the present to another aspect of
it, closely allied with the remote past, from
the enlightened advocate of natural Science
to the apologist for antiquated and gross
superstition, from the author of *Scepsis
Scientifica* and *Plus Ultra* to the writer

of *Sadducismus Triumphatus; or, a Full
and Plain Evidence concerning Witches and
Apparitions.* Such a conjunction is, however, not unparalleled. Many instances
occur both among ancient and modern
thinkers of a cautious skepticism in one
direction being counterbalanced by a sur-
plusage of faith in another. Nor is
Glanvill's philosophical suspense totally
unrelated to his witch-beliefs. Skepticism,
we must remember, is largely a cleansing
process, and may possibly result in the
admission into the swept and garnished
intellect of some other spirits more wicked
than the single one exorcised. He indeed
calls attention to the connexion between his
Scepsis and his Book on Witches (*Sad.
Tri.* p. 7), the plea for the existence of such
supernatural beings as witches being based
on that very ignorance of the hidden
processes of Nature which it is the object of
the *Scepsis* to set forth and demonstrate.
There are besides other points of connexion
between this superstition of Glanvill's and
his general environment and mental confor-
mation. With all his desire to emancipate
himself from the Puritanism of the Commonwealth, his thought betrays occasional sym-

d

pathies with its origin, as we have already incidentally noted. Here, at least, he is in full accord with the despised Sectaries. No article of Puritan faith was more firmly grounded than that which related to the reality and malefic power of witches, and Glanvill's work on the subject is only one of a large number written by "enthusiasts" and Sectaries whose other *credenda* he would have disdainfully rejected. No doubt the dominating element in his intellectual formation was not Sentiment nor Intuition, but Reason. Still, it was Reason qualified by emotional sensitiveness, as well as by an eager powerful imagination, which sometimes carried him further than he wanted to go. His "warm, spruce and gay fancy" is apparent in all his works, even in those which treat of science and philosophy ; but in no direction does he allow it freer flight than within the confines of the spirit world. We must therefore find in his uncompromising belief in the existence and perpetual activity of non-material Beings a primary motive of his witch-faith. But the work had also a polemical object. It was written to confute the materialists of his time. "'Tis well known," he says, "that the Sadducees denied the existence of spirits and the Immortality of Souls, and the heresie is sadly revived in our days." (*Essay* iv. p. 8). On the truth of the latter statement it is needless to dilate. All who are acquainted with the chief undercurrents of English speculation during the latter half of Charles II.'s reign are aware that not the least influential among them was an unthinking and gross materialism, —which was in itself, let us add, only the natural reaction of Puritan dogmatism—as to the manifold activities of the world of spirits. This materialism Glanvill attacks in the most vehement fashion. Not only was the denial of spirits unjustifiable, but it was unphilosophical. It set an absolute barrier to speculation. It asserted a finality which was both arbitrary and incapable of proof, and it left many unquestioned facts in human history without any rational basis. But once the existence and continuous energy of good spirits were admitted, then, according to Glanvill, there must needs be bad spirits as well, and their activities will probably be no less varied. The inference, though in an opposite direction, was precisely that by which Göethe's Supernaturalist on the Brocken inferred the existence of good spirits :

> " Denn von den Teufeln kann ich ja
> Auf Gute Geister schliessen."

We have no space to dwell further on Glanvill's " Vanquished Sadducieism," nor to resuscitate the Demon of Tedworth and other fantastic spectres of equal authenticity from the oblivion which is their just due. The argument of the book is in form Inductive. Glanvill bases his proof on what he terms a choice *collection* of modern Relations, but it is in truth a travesty of the Inductive method, and betrays a ludicrous misconception of the nature of human testimony. But while we assign to Glanvill's witch-beliefs their merited estimate, we must remember that we cannot fairly blame him for not being in advance of his time. His benighted condition on this subject was shared by most of his compeers in English thought. Boyle, Henry More, Meric Casaubon, Baxter, Cudworth, all believed fully in Witchcraft, and most of them wrote in its defence. Glanvill's own co-Fellows of the Royal Society were similarly fully persuaded of the truth of Alchymy, and in some cases attested their scientific instincts by a diligent search for the philosopher's stone. Bacon himself believed in the transmutation of metals, and Sir Kenelm Digby's sympathetic powder and weapon salve found numerous recipients as credulous as their author. On the whole, then, while we cannot exonerate the author of the *Scepsis* from sharing an unworthy and degrading superstition, we must allow him the extenuating circumstances which are always due when a man's errors are the outcome of his environment. After all, a thinker's claim to stand in the forefront of the speculation of his time must be determined not by an impossible freedom from all the errors by which he is surrounded, but by such a comparative immunity from some of them, as enables him to reach forward to, and represent the Knowledge and enlightenment of the Future. Readers of the *Scepsis*, the *Plus Ultra*, and the collected "*Essays*," will have no difficulty in claiming such a position for Joseph Glanvill.

Our space rather than the interest of the subject is exhausted. All we have attempted is to set before the readers of the ensuing treatise, such particulars as to the life and thought of its author as seemed likely to enhance their appreciation of his work, and to aid its fuller comprehension. Let us add, that the spirit and intent of Glanvill's work seems to us of more durable worth than its form, though this also is charged with manifold interest. As long as men are constituted as they are, the peace and welfare of the world will always be imperilled by excessive dogma, or too confident Belief on many moot points of speculation, not only in Philosophy and Theology, but in Science, Politics, and other departments of human thought which deal with indeterminable matters and issues, and therefore there will always be room for a Scientific Skepticism—for the enquiry and judicial suspense of the truly wise man.

AN ADDRESS, &c.

TO THE

ROYAL SOCIETY.

Illustrious Gentlemen,

T*HE name of your Honorable* Society *is so* August *and* Glorious, *and this trifle to which I have prefixt it, of so mean, and so unsuitable a quality ; that 'tis fit I should give an account of an action so seemingly* obnoxious. *And I can expect no other from those, that judge by* first sights *and* rash measures, *then to be thought* fond *or* insolent ; *or, as one that hath* unmeet thoughts *of himself, or YOU. But if a* naked profession *may have credit in a case wherein no other evidence can be given of an* intention ; *I adventured not on this Address upon the usual* Motives *of* Dedications. *It was not upon design to credit these Papers (which yet derive much* accidental *Honour from the occasion.) Nor to complement a* Society *so much above* Flattery, *and the regardless air of* common Applauses. *I intended not your*

Illustrious Name *the dishonour of being* Fence *against* detraction *for a performance, which possibly deserves it.* Nor *was it to* publish *how much I* honour *You* ; *which were to fancy my self considerable.* Much *less was I so fond, to think I could contribute any thing to a* Constellation *of* Worthies *from whom the Learned World expects to be informed.* But, *considering how much it is the interest of Mankinde in order to the* advance *of* Knowledge, *to be sensible they have not yet attain'd it* ; *or at least, but in* poor *and* diminutive measures ; *and regarding Your* Society *as the strongest* Argument *to perswade a* modest *and* reserved diffidence *in opinions, I took the boldness to borrow that deservedly celebrated* name, *for an* evidence *to my Subject* ; *that so what was wanting in my* Proof, *might be made up in the* Example. *For If we were yet arriv'd to* certain *and* infallible *Accounts in Nature, from whom might we more reasonably expect them then from a Number of Men, whom, their impartial* Search, *wary* Procedure, *deep* Sagacity, *twisted* Endeavours, *ample* Fortunes, *and all other advantages, have rendered infinitely more likely to have succeeded in those Enquiries* ; *then the* sloth, haste, *and* babble *of talking* Disputants ; *or the greatest industry of* single *and less qualified Attempters ? If therefore those (whom, I am in no danger of being disbelieved by any that understand the world and them, if I call the most learned and ingenious Society in* Europe.*) if they, I say, confess the* narrowness *of* humane attainments, *and dare not* confide *in the most plausible of their* Sentiments ; *if such great and instructed Spirits think we have not as yet* Phænomena *enough to make as much as* Hypotheseis ; *much less, to fix* certain Laws *and prescribe* Methods *to Nature in her Actings : what insolence is it then in the lesser* size *of Mortals, who possibly know nothing but what they glean'd from some little* Systeme, *or the* Disputes *of Men that love to swagger for Opinions, to boast* Infallibility *of* Knowledge, *and* swear *they see the* Sun *at* Midnight !

Nor was this the only inducement to the dishonour I have done you in the direction of these worthless Papers ; *But I must confess I design'd hereby to serve my self in another interest. For having been so hardy as to undertake a charge against the* Philosophy *of the* Schools, *and to attempt upon a* name *which among some is yet very* Sacred, *I was lyable to have been overborne by a* Torrent *of* Authorities, *and to have had the voyce of my* single reason *against* it, *drown'd in the noise of* Multitudes *of* Applauders : *That I might not therefore be vapour'd down by* Insignificant Testimonies, *or venture* bare reasons *against what the doating world counts more valuable, I presumed to use the great* Name *of your* Society *to* annihilate *all such* arguments. *And I cannot think that any, that is but* indifferently *impudent, will have the confidence to urge, either the* greatness *of the* Authour, *or the* number *of its* Admirers *in behalf of that* Philosophy, *after the ROYAL SOCIETY is mention'd. For though your Honourable and ingenious* Assembly *hath not so little to do, as to Dispute with Men that count it a great attainment to be able to talk much, and little to the purpose : And though you have not thought it worth your labour to enter a profess'd dissent against a Philosophy which the greatest part of the* Virtuosi, *and* enquiring spirits *of* Europe *have deserted, as a meer* maze *of* words, *and* useless contrivance : *Yet the credit which the* Mathematicks *have with you, your* experimental *way of* Enquiry, *and* Mechanical Attempts *for solving the* Phænomena ; *be-*

sides that some of you (to whose excellent
works the learned world is deeply indebted)
publickly own the Cartesian and Atomical
Hypotheseis ; These, I say, are arguments of
your no great favour to the Aristotelian.
For indeed that disputing physiology is of no
accommodation to your designs ; which are
not to teach Men to cant endlessly about
Materia, and Forma ; to hunt Chimæra's by
rules of Art, or to dress up Ignorance in
words of bulk and sound, which shall stop
the mouth of enquiry, and make learned fools
seem Oracles among the populace : But the
improving the minds of Men in solid and
useful notices of things, helping them to such
Theories as may be serviceable to common
life, and the searching out the true laws of
Matter and Motion, in order to the securing
of the Foundations of Religion against all
attempts of Mechanical Atheism.

In order to the Furtherance (according to
my poor measure) of which great and worthy
purposes, these Papers were first intended.
For perceiving that several ingenious persons whose assistance might be conducive to
the Advance of real and useful Knowledge,
lay under the prejudices of Education and
Customary Belief ; I thought that the en-

larging them to a state of more generous Freedom by striking at the root of Pedantry *and* opinionative Assurance *would be no hinderance to the Worlds improvement. For Such it was then that the ensuing* Essay *was designed; which therefore wears a dress, that possibly is not so suitable to the graver* Geniusses, *who have outgrown all* gayeties *of* style *and* youthful relishes ; *But yet perhaps is not improper for the persons, for whom it was prepared. And there is nothing in* words *and* styles *but* suitableness, *that makes them* acceptable *and* effective. *If therefore this Discourse, such as it is, may tend to the removal of any* accidental *disadvantages from* capable Ingenuities, *and the preparing them for* inquiry, *I know you have so noble an* ardour *for the benefit of Mankind, as to pardon a* weak *and* defective *performance to a* laudable *and* well-directed *intention. And though, if you were acted by the spirit of common Mortals, you need not care for the propagation of that* gallantry *and* intellectual grandeur *which you are so eminently owners of, since 'tis a greater* credit, *and possibly* pleasure, *to be* wise *when* few are *so ; yet* you *being no Factors for Glory or* Treasure, *but* disinterested Attempters *for the* universal good, *cannot but favourably regard any thing, that in the least degree may do the considering World a kindness;* and to enoble it with the spirit that inspires the *ROYAL SOCIETY, were to advantage it in one of the best Capacities in which it is improveable.* These Papers then (as I have intimated) having been directed to an End subordinate to this, viz. the disposing the less stupid *Minds for that honour and improvement;* I thought it very proper to call up their eyes to you, and to fix them on their Example: *That so* natural Ambition *might take part with* reason and their *interest to encourage* imitation. In order to which, I think it needless to endeavour to celebrate you in a profest Encomium; since customary Strains and affected Juvenilities have made it difficult to commend, and speak credibly in Dedications; And your deserts, impossible in this. So that he that undertakes it, must either be wanting to your merits, or speak things that will find but little credit among those that do not know You. Or, possibly such, as will be interpreted only as what of course is said on such occasions, rather because 'tis usual, then because 'tis just. But the splendour of a Society, illus-

trious both by blood *and* vertue, *excuseth my Pen from a* subject, *in which it must either* appear vain, *or* be defective. *I had much rather take notice therefore, how* providentially *you are met together in Dayes, wherein people of* weak Heads *on the one hand, and* vile affections *on the other, have made an* unnatural divorce *between being* Wise *and* Good. These *conceiving* Reason *and* Philosophy *sufficient* vouchees *of* Licentious practices *and their secret* scorn of Religion ; *and Those reckoning it a great instance of* Piety *and devout* Zeal, vehemently *to declaim against* Reason *and* Philosophy. *And what result can be expected from such supposals, That 'tis a piece of* Wit *and* Gallantry *to be an* Atheist, *and of* Atheism *to be a* Philosopher, *but* Irreligion *on the one side, and* Superstition *on the other, which will end in open irreclaimeable* Atheism *on* both ? *Now it seems to me a signality in* Providence *in erecting your most* Honourable Society *in such a juncture of* dangerous Humours, *the very mention of which is evidence, that* Atheism *is* impudent *in pretending to* Philosophy ; *And* Superstition *sottishly* ignorant *in phancying, that the* knowledge *of* Nature *tends to* Irreligion. *But to leave this latter*

to it's conceits, and the little impertinencies
of humour and folly it is fond of : The
former is more dangerous, though not more
reasonable. For where 'tis once presumed,
that the whole Fabrick of Religion is built
upon Ignorance of the Nature of things ;
And the belief of a God, ariseth from un-
acquaintance with the Laws of Matter and
Motion ; what can be the issue of such presumptions, but that those that are so perswaded, should desire to be wise in a way that
will gratifie their Appetites : And so give
up themselves to the swinge of their unbounded propensions? Yea, and those, the
impiety of whose lives makes them regret a
Deity, and secretly wish there were none
will greedily listen to a Doctrine that strikes
at the existence of a Being, the sense of
whom is a restraint and check upon the
licence of their Actions. And thus all
wickedness and debauches will flow in upon
the world like a mighty deluge, and beat
down all the Banks of Laws, Vertue, and
Sobriety before them.

Now though few have yet arrived to that
pitch of Impiety, or rather Folly, openly to
own such sentiments ; yet, I doubt, this con-
cealment derives rather from the fear of

Man, *then from the* love *or* fear *of any Being* above him. *And what the* confident *exploding of all* immaterial Substances, *the* unbounded prerogatives *are bestowed upon* Matter, *and the* consequent assertions, *signifie, you need not be informed. I could wish there were less reason to suspect them branches of a dangerous* Cabbala. *For the ingenious* World *being grown quite weary of* Qualities *and* Formes, *and declaring in favour of the* Mechanical Hypothesis, *(to which a person that is not very fond of* Religion *is a great pretender) divers of the brisker* Geniusses, *who desire rather to be accounted* Witts, *then endeavour to* be so, *have been willing to accept* Mechanism *upon* Hobbian *conditions, and many others were in danger of following them into the* pre-cipice. *So that 'tis not conceivable how a more suitable* remedy *could have been provided against the* deadly influence *of that* Contagion, *then your Honourable* Society, *by which the meanest intellects may perceive, that* Mechanick Philosophy *yields no security to* irreligion, *and that those that would be* gentilely *learned and ingenious, need not purchase it, at the* dear *rate of being* Atheists. *Nor can the* prolep-

tical notions *of Religion be so well
defended by the* profest Servants *of the*
Altar, *who usually suppose them, and are
less furnished with* advantages *for such*
speculations ; *so that* their *Attempts in this
kind will be interpreted by such as are not
willing to be convinced, as the* products *of*
interest, *or* ignorance *in* Mechanicks ; *which
suspicions can never be deriv'd upon a*
Society *of persons of* Quality *and* Honour,
who are embodied *for no other* interest *but
that of the* Publique, *and whose abilities in
this kind are too* bright *to admit the least*
shadow *of the other* Censure. *And 'tis to
be hoped, that the* eminence *of your* condition, *and the* gallantry *of your* Principles,
which are worthy *those that own them, will
invite Gentlemen to the* useful *and* enobling
study of Nature, *and make* Philosophy
fashionable ; *whereas while that which the
World call'd* so, *consisted of nought but* dry
Spinosities, lean Notions, *and* endless Alterations *about things of* nothing, *all unbecom-
ing Men of* generous Spirit *and* Education ;
of use *no where but where folkes are bound
to* talk *by a* Law, *and profest by few but
persons of* ordinary *condition ; while, I say,*
Philosophy *was of* such *a* nature, *and*

cloathed *with such* circumstances, *how could it be otherwise then* contemptible, *in the esteem of the more* enfranchised *and* sprightly *tempers?* *So that your* Illustrious Society *hath* redeemed *the* credit *of* Philosophy; *and I hope to see it accounted a piece of none of the* meanest breeding *to be acquainted with the* Laws *of* Nature *and the* Universe. *And doubtless there is nothing wherein men of* birth *and* fortune *would better consult their* treble interest *of PLEASURE, ESTATE, and HONOUR, then by such* generous researches. *In which* (1.) *they'l find all the innocent* satisfactions *which use to follow* victory, variety, *and* surprise, *the usual sources of our best tasted* pleasures. *And perhaps* humane nature *meets few more* sweetly relishing *and* cleanly joyes, *then those, that derive from the* happy issues *of* successful Tryals : *Yea, whether they succeed to the answering the particular* aim *of the* Naturalist *or not* ; *'tis however a* pleasant *spectacle to behold the* shifts, windings *and* unexpected Caprichios of *distressed* Nature, *when pursued by a* close *and* well managed Experiment. *And the* delights *which result from these* nobler entertainments *are such,* as our cool *and* reflecting thoughts *need not be* ashamed *of. And which are dogged by no such sad sequels as are the products of those* titillations *that reach no higher then* Phancy *and the* Senses. *And* that *alone deserves to be call'd* so, *which is* pleasure *without* guilt *or* pain. *Nor* (2.) *have the* frugaller Sons *of* fortune *any reason to object the* Costliness *of the* delights *we speak of, since, in all likelyhood, they frequently* pay dearer *for less* advantagious pleasures. *And it may be there are few better wayes of* adding *to what they are affraid to* waste, *then* inquiries *into* Nature. *For by a* skilful application *of those* notices, *may be gain'd in such* researches, *besides the* accelerating *and* bettering *of* Fruits, emptying Mines, drayning Fens *and* Marshes, *which may hereby be* effected, *at much more* easie *and* less expensive rates, *then by the* common methods *of such* performances : *I say, besides these,* Lands *may be* advanced *to scarce credible* degrees *of* improvement, *and innumerable other* advantages *may be* obtain'd *by an* industry *directed by* Philosophy *and* Mechanicks, *which can never be expected from* drudging Ignorance. *But though those* inquisitive pursuits *of* things *should make out no pretence to* Pleasure *or* Advantage ; *yet upon the last Account* (3.) *of Honour, they are* infinitely recommendable *to all that have any* sense *of such an* interest. *For 'tis a* greater credit, *if we judge by equal measures, to* understand *the* Art *whereby the* Almighty Wisdom *governs the* Motions *of the great* Automaton, *and to know the wayes of* captivating Nature, *and making her* subserve *our* purposes *and* designments ; *then to have* learnt *all the* intrigues *of* Policy, *and the* Cabals *of* States *and* King-doms ; *yea, then to* triumph *in the* head *of* victorious Troops *over* conquer'd Empires. *Those* successes *being more* glorious *which bring* benefit *to the World; then such* ruinous ones *as are dyed in* humane blood, *and* cloathed *in the* livery *of* Cruelty *and* Slaughter.

Nor are these all the advantages *upon the Account of which we owe* acknowledgments *to* Providence *for your* erection ; *since from your* promising *and* generous endeavours, *we may hopefully expect a considerable* in-largement *of the* History *of* Nature, *without which our* Hypotheseis *are but* Dreams *and* Romances, *and our* Science *meer* conjecture *and* opinion. *For while we frame* Scheames *of* things *without consulting the* Phænomena, *we do but* build *in the* Air, *and* describe *an* Imaginary World *of our* own making, *that is but little a kin to the* real one *that* God made. *And 'tis possible that all the* Hypotheseis *that yet have been contrived,* were *built upon too narrow an* inspection *of* things, *and the* phasies *of the* Universe. *For the advancing* day *of* experimental knowledge *discloseth such* appearances, *as will not lye* even, *in any* model *extant. And perhaps the newly discovered* Ring *about* Saturn, *to mention no more, will scarce be accounted for by any* systeme *of things the World hath yet been acquainted with. So that little can be looked for towards the* advancement *of* natural Theory, *but from those, that are likely to mend our* prospect *of* events *and* sensible appearances ; *the defect of which will suffer us to proceed no further towards* Science, *then to* imperfect guesses, *and* timerous supposals. *And from whom can this* great *and* noble Acquist *be expected, if not from a* Society *of persons that can command both* Wit *and* Fortune *to serve them, and professedly ingage* both *in* experimental *pursuits of* Nature ?

The desired success *of which kind of ingagements cannot so reasonably be looked for from any in the known* Universe, *as from your most Honourable* Society, *where* fondness *of* preconceiv'd opinions, sordid Interests, *or* affectation *of* strange Relations, *are not like to render your* reports suspect *or* partial, *nor want of* Sagacity, Fortune, *or* Care, *defective : some of which possibly have been* ingredients *in most former* experiments. *So that the relations of your* Tryals *may be received as undoubted* Records *of* certain events, *and as securely be depended on, as the* Propositions *of* Euclide. *Which* advantage *cannot be hoped from* private undertakers, *or* Societies *less qualified and conspicuous then* Yours. *And how great a benefit such a* Natural History *as may be confided in, will prove to the whole stock of* learned Mankinde, *those that understand the interest of the* inquiring World *may conjecture. Doubtless, the success of those your* great *and* Catholick Endeavours *will promote the* Empire *of* Man *over* Nature ; *and bring plentiful accession of* Glory *to your* Nation ; *making* BRITAIN *more justly famous then the once celebrated* GREECE ;

and LONDON *the* wiser ATHENS. *For* You really *are what former Ages could contrive but in* wish *and* Romances; *and* Solomons House *in the* NEW ATLANTIS *was a Prophetick Scheam of the* ROYAL SOCIETY. *And though such* August *designs as inspire your enquiries, use to be derided by* drolling phantasticks, *that have only wit enough to make others and themselves* ridiculous : *Yet there's no reproach in the scoffs of* Ignorance ; *and those that are wise enough to understand* your worth, *and the* merit *of* your endeavours, *will contemn the* silly taunts *of* fleering Buffoonry ; *and the* jerks *of that* Wit, *that is but a kind of* confident, *and* well-acted folly. *And 'tis none of the least considerable expectations that may be reasonably had of your* Society, *that 'twill discredit that* toyishness *of* wanton fancy ; *and pluck the misapplyed name of the* WITS, *from those conceited* Humourists *that have assum'd it ; to bestow it upon the more* manly spirit *and* genius, *that playes not tricks with* words, *nor frolicks with the* Caprices *of* froathy imagination : *But imployes a* severe reason *in enquiries into the momentous concernments of the* Universe.

On consideration of all which Accounts, *I think it* just *you should have acknowledgments from all the* Sons *and* Favourers *of* Wisdom : *and I cannot believe it a crime for me to own my part of those obligations (though in a* slender offering) *for which all the thoughtful and awakened World is your* debtour ; *no more then 'twas a fault to pay the* tribute penny *to* Cæsar, *or is a piece of* guilt *to be* dutiful. *And though perhaps I have not so well consulted the repute of my* intellectuals, *in bringing their* weaknesses *and* imperfections *into such* discerning presences ; *yet I am well content, if thereby I have given any proof of an* honest will, *and wellmeaning* Morals ; *And I think, I can without repugnance Sacrifice the* former, *to an occasion of gaining myself this* latter *and* better *Testimony ; of which disposition, I say, I am now giving an instance in presenting so* Illustrious *an* Assembly *with a* Discourse, *that hath nothing to recommend it, but the* devotion *wherewith 'tis offer'd them. And really when I compare this* little *and* mean performance, *with the* vastness *of my* subject ; *I am* discourag'd *by the* disproportion : *And me thinks I have*

brought but a Cockle-shell *of water from the*
Ocean : *Whatever I look upon within the*
amplitude *of* heaven *and* earth, *is evidence
of* humane ignorance ; *For all things are a*
great darkness *to us, and we are* so *unto
our selves : The* plainest *things are as*
obscure, *as the most confessedly* mysterious ;
and the Plants *we tread on, are as much*
above *us, as the* Stars *and* Heavens. *The
things that* touch *us are as* distant *from us,
as the* Pole ; *and we are as much* strangers
to our selves, *as to the inhabitants of*
America. *On review of which, me thinks
I could begin a new to describe the* poverty
of our intellectual acquisitions, *and the*
vanity *of* bold opinion ; *Which the* Dogmatists *themselves demonstrate in all the
controversies they are engaged in ; each party
being* confident *that the others* confidence *is*
vain ; *from which a* third *may more reasonably conclude the* same *of the* confidence *of*
both. *And methinks there should need no
more to reduce* disputing *men to* modest
*acknowledgments, and more becoming temper,
then the consideration ; That there is not
any thing about which the* reason *of Man
is capable of being imployed, but hath been*

the subject *of* Dispute, *and* diversity *of* apprehension. *So that, as the excellent Lord* Mountaigne *hath observed,* [Mankind is agreed in nothing ; no, not in this, that the heavens are over us ;] every man *almost* differing *from* another ; *Yea, and* every man *from* himself : *And yet* every man *is* assur'd *of his own* Scheams *of* conjecture, *though he cannot hold this* assurance, *but by this* proud absurdity, *That he alone is in the right, and all the rest of the World mistaken. I say then, there being so much to be produced both from the* natural *and* moral *World to the* shame *of* boasting Ignorance ; *the ensuing Treatise, which with a* timerous *and* unassur'd countenance *adventures into your* presence, *can pride it self in no higher title, then that of an ESSAY, or imperfect offer at a Subject, to which it could not do right but by discoursing all things. On which consideration, I had once resolv'd to suffer this Trifle to pass both out of* Print *and* Memory ; *But another thought suggesting, that the* instances *I had given of* humane Ignorance *were not only* clear *ones, but* such *as are not so ordinarily* suspected ; *from which to our* shortness *in most things else, 'tis an* easie inference, *and* a potiori, *I was perswaded, and somewhat by* experience, *that it might not be altogether* unuseful *in the capacities 'twas intended for: And on these Accounts I suffer'd this* Publication ; *to which (without vanity I speak it) I found so faint an inclination, that I could have been well content to suffer it to have slipt into the state of* eternal silence *and* oblivion. *For I must confess that* way *of* writing *to be less agreeable to my* present relish *and* Genius ; *which is more gratified with* manly sense, *flowing in a* natural *and* unaffected Eloquence, *then in the* musick *and curiosity of* fine Metaphors *and* dancing periods. *To which measure of my present humour, I had indeavour'd to reduce the style of these Papers ; but that I was loth to give my self that trouble in an Affair, to which I was grown too* cold *to be* much *concern'd in. And this* inactivity *of temper perswaded me, I might reasonably expect a pardon from the* ingenious, *for* faults *committed in an* immaturity *of* Age *and* Judgment *that would excuse them ; and perhaps I may have still need to plead it to atone for the imperfections of this* Address :

By which, though I have exposed deformities *to the clearest* Sunshine, *that some others prudence would have directed into the* shades *and more* private recesses ; *Yet I am secure to lose nothing by the adventure that is comparably valued by me as is the Honour of declaring my self,*

Illustrious Gentlemen,

The most humble Admirer

of Your August Society,

Jos. Glanvill.

SCEPSIS SCIENTIFICA;

OR,

THE VANITY OF DOGMATIZING.

SCEPSIS SCIENTIFICA;

OR,

THE VANITY OF DOGMATIZING.

CHAP. I.

A general Description of the state of Primitive Ignorance ; *by way of* Introduction.

WHATever is the *Innocence* and *Infelicity* of the present *state*, we cannot, without affronting the *Divine Goodness*, deny, but that at first we were made *wise* and *happy;* For nothing of *specifick imperfection* or deformity could come from the hands that were directed by an *Almighty Wisdome;* so that, whatever disorders have since befallen them, all things were at first disposed by an *Omniscient Intellect* that cannot contrive *ineptly;* and our selves exactly formed according to the *Idæa's* of that *Mind*, which frames things consonantly to the Rules of their respective Natures. But a particular knowledge of the

A

blest advantages, and happy circumstances
of our primitive condition, is lost with *Innocence ;* and there are scarce any hints of
conjecture from the *present.* How ever, this
perhaps we may safely venture on by way of
general Description ;

That the *Æternal Wisdome* from which
we derive our beings, inrich't us with
all those enoblements that were suitable
to the measures of an unstraightned *Goodness,* and the *capacity* of such a *kind*
of Creature.   And as the *primogenial*
Light which at first was diffused over
the face of the unfashion'd *Chaos,* was
afterwards contracted into the Fountain *Lu-
minaryes ;* so those scattered perfections
which were divided among the several ranks
of inferiour Natures, were summ'd up, and
constellated in *ours.* Thus the then happy
temper of our condition and affairs anti-
cipated the Aspires to be *Like Gods;* and
possibly was scarce to be added to as much
as in desire.   But the unlikeness of it to our
now *miserable,* because *Apostate,* State,
makes it almost as impossible to be *conceiv'd,* as to be *regained.* 'Twas a condition
envied by Creatures that nature had placed
a Sphear above us ; and such as differ'd not

much from *Glory* and blessed *Immortality* but in *perpetuity* and *duration*.

For since the most despicable and dis-regarded pieces of decayed nature are so curiously wrought, and adorned with such eminent signatures of Divine *Wisdome* as speak *It* their Authour, and that after a Curse brought upon a disorder'd Universe : with how rich an *Embroydery* then think we were the nobler composures dignified in the days of spotless Innocence? And of how sublime a quality were the *perfections* of the Creature that was to wear the *Image* of the Prime *perfection?* Doubtless, they were as much above the *Hyperbolies* that Fond Poetry bestowes upon it's admired objects, as their flatter'd imperfect beauties are really below them. And the most refined Glories of *Subcælestial* excellencies are but more faint resemblances of *these.* For all the powers and faculties of this *Copy* of the *Divinity*, this *Meddal* of *God*, were as perfect, as *beauty* and *harmony* in *Idæa.* The *soul* being not cloy'd by an unactive mass, as *now ;* nor hindered in it's actings, by the *distemperature* of indisposed Organs, *Passions* kept their place, and transgrest not the boundaries of their proper Natures ;

Nor were the disorders began which are occasion'd by the licence of unruly *Appetites.* Now though perhaps some will not allow such vast advantages to the *terrestrial Adam*, which they think not consistent with the *History*, and circumstances of his *Defection :* Yet those that suppose the *Allegory* and *Præexistence*, will easily admit all this, and more of the *Æthereal* Condition. But I'le not determine any thing in matters of so high and difficult a Nature ; which ever is the truth, this general Accompt I have given is not concerned ; I asserting only what both will acknowledge, That the first condition of our natures was a state of blessedness and perfection.

CHAP. II.

Our Decay and Ruines by the Fall *; particularly those of our Intellectual Powers.*

BUT, 'tis a *miserable* thing to *have* been *happy.* And a self contracted wretchedness, is a double one. Had *Felicity* alwayes been a stranger to our natures, our *now misery* had been *none ;* And had not our selves been the Authours of our Ruines, *less.* We might have been *made unhappy*, but since we are *miserable* we *chose* it. He that gave them, might have taken from us our other enjoyments, but nothing could have rob'd us of *innocence* but our *selves.* That we are below the Angels of God is no *misery*, tis the *lot* of our *Natures :* But that we have made our selves like the *beasts that perish*, is severely *so*, because the Fruit of a voluntary defection. While Man was *innocent* he was likely *ignorant* of nothing, that imported him to know. But when he had *transgrest*, the Fault that opened his eyes upon his *shame*, shut them up from most things else, but his newly purchased *misery.* He saw the *Nakedness* of his *soul* with that of his *body*, and the blindness and disarray of his Faculties, which his former innocence was a stranger to. And what disclosed this *Poverty* and these *Disorders*, caused them, whether the *understanding* and *affections* were the most criminal Authours of that unhappy defailance, need not be disputed. And how evils should commence in so blessed a Constitution of affairs, and advantageous temper of them · both, will perhaps difficultly be determined : Merciful Heaven having made it easier to know the *cure*, then the *rise* of our distempers. This is certain, that our *Masculine powers* are deeply sharers of the consequential mischiefs ; and though *Eve* were the first in the *disobedience*, yet was *Adam* a joynt partaker of the *Curse :* So that we are not now like the Creatures we were made, but have lost both our Makers *image*, and our own. And possibly the Beasts are not more inferiour to us, then we are to our antient selves : A proud affecting to be like *Gods* having made us unlike *Men.* For (to pass the other instances of our degradation which indeed were a plentiful Subject, but not so press to my design) our *intellectual* and Highest *Faculties* are deplorable evidence of our Ruins. And upon these I shall fix my Observations.

For whereas our ennobled understandings could once take the wings of the morning, to visit the World above us, and had a glorious display of the highest form of created excellencies, they now lye groveling in this lower region, muffled up in mists, and darkness : the curse of the Serpent is fallen upon *degenerated* Man, *To go on his belly and lick the dust.* And as in the

Cartesian hypothesis, the Planets sometimes lose their light, by the fixing of the impurer *scum;* so our impared intellectuals, which were once as pure *light and flame* in regard of their vigour and activity, are now darkned by those grosser *spots*, which disobedience hath contracted. And our now overshadow'd souls (to whose beauties Stars were foils) may be exactly emblem'd, by those *crusted globes*, whose influential emissions are intercepted, by the interposal of the benighting element, while the purer essence is imprison'd by the gross and impervious Matter. For these once glorious lights, which did freely shed abroad their harmless beams, and wanton'd in a larger circumference, are now pent up in a few *first principles* (the *naked essentials* of our *faculties*) within the straight confines of a Prison. And whereas knowledge dwelt in our undepraved natures, as light in the *Sun*, in as great plenty, as purity ; it is now hidden in us like sparks in a flint, both in scarcity and obscurity.

For, considering the *shortness* of our *intellectual sight*, the *deceptibility* and impositions of our *senses*, the tumultuary *disorders* of our *passions*, the *prejudices* of

our *infant educations*, and infinite such like
(of which an after occasion will befriend us,
with a more full and particular recital) I say,
by reason of these, we may conclude of the
science of the most of men, truly so called,
that it may be truss'd up in the same room
with the *Iliads*, yea it may be all the
certainty of those high pretenders to it, the
voluminous Schoolmen, and Peripatetical
Dictators, (bating what they have of the first
Principles and the Word of God) may be
circumscribed by as small a circle, as the
Creed, when *Brachygraphy* had confined it
within the compass of a penny. And methinks the disputes of those assuming
confidents, that think so highly of their
Attainments, are like the controversie of
those in *Plato's* den, who having never seen
but the shadow of an horse trajected against
a wall, eagerly contended, whether its *neigh-
ing* proceeded from the appearing Mane, or
Tail, ruffled with the winds. And the
Dogmatist's are no less at odds in the
darker cells of their *imaginary* Principles
about the *shaddows* and *exuviæ* of beings ;
when for the most part they are strangers to
the substantial *Realities*. And like children
are very buisie about the Babyes of their

Phancies, while their useless subtilties afford little entertainment to the nobler Faculties.

But many of the most accomplish't wits of all ages, whose modesty would not allow them to boast of more then they were owners of, have resolv'd their knowledge into *Socrates* his summe total, and after all their pains in quest of *Science*, have sat down in a professed *nescience*. It is the shallow unimproved intellects that are confident pretenders to certainty ; as if contrary to the *Adage*, *Science had no friend but Ignorance*. And though their general acknowledgments of the weakness of *humane understanding*, and the *narrowness* of what we know, look like *cold* and *sceptical* discouragements ; yet the particular expressions of their *sentiments* and *opinions*, are as *Oracular*, as if they were *Omniscient*. To such, as a curb to confidence, and as an evidence of humane infirmities even in the noblest parts of Man, I shall give the following instances of our intellectual blindness : not that I intend to poze them with those common *Ænigma's* of *Magnetism*, *Fluxes*, *Refluxes*, and the like ; these are resolv'd into a *confest* ignorance and I shall not persue them to their old *Asylum ;* and yet it may be there is more knowable in these, then in less acknowledg'd mysteries : But I'le not move beyond our selves, and the most ordinary and trivial *Phænomena* in nature, in which we shall find enough to shame *Confidence,* and unplume *Dogmatizing.*

CHAP. III.

A general Account of our Ignorance of our own Natures.

TO begin then with the *Theory* of our own *Natures;* we shall find in them too great evidence of *intellectual* deficience and deplorable confessions of *humane igno-rance.* For we came into the world, and we *know* not *how;* we live in't in a *self-nescience,* and go hence again and are as ignorant of our *recess.* We *grow,* we *live,* we *move* at first in a *Microcosm,* and can give no more *Scientifical* account, of the state of our three *quarters* confinement, then if we had never been extant in the greater world, but had expir'd in an *abortion;* we are enlarg'd from the prison of the womb, our *sences* are affected, we *imagine* and *remember;* and yet

know no more of the *immediate* reasons of
these common functions, then those little
Embryo Anchorites: We *breath*, we *talk*, we
move, while we are ignorant of the manner
of these vital performances. The *Dogmatist*
knows not how he stirs his finger ; nor by
what art or method he directs his tongue in
articulating *sounds* into *voyces*. *New* parts
are added to our substance, to supply our
continual *decayings*, and as we *dye* we are
born dayly ; nor can we give a certain account, how the *aliment* is so prepared for
nutrition, or by what *mechanism* it is so
regularly distributed ; we are transported by
Passions; and our *mindes* ruffled by the
disorders of the *body;* Nor yet can we tell
how these should reach our *immaterial
selves*, or how the *Soul* should be affected by
such kind of *agitations.* We lay us down,
to *sleep* away our cares ; night shuts up the
Senses windows, the mind contracts into the
Brains *centre;* We *live* in *death*, and *lye* as
in the *grave.* Now we know nothing, nor
can our waking thoughts inform us, who is
Morpheus, and what that leaden *Key* is that
locks us up within our senseless Cels :
There's a difficulty that pincheth, nor will it
easily be resolved. The Soul is awake, and

solicited by external motions, for some of
them reach the perceptive region in the
most silent repose, and obscurity of night.
What is't then that prevents our *Sensations;*
or if we do perceive, how is't that we *know
it not?* But we *Dream,* see *Visions,* converse with *Chimæra's;* the one half of our
lives is a *Romance,* a fiction. We retain a
catch of those pretty stories, and our
awakened imagination smiles in the recol-
lection. Nor yet can our most severe inquiries finde what did so abuse us, or show
the nature and manner of these nocturnal
illusions: When we puzzle our selves in the
disquisition, we do but *dream,* and every
Hypothesis is a *phancy.* Our most industrious conceits are but like their object, and
as uncertain as those of midnight. Thus
when some dayes and nights have gone over
us, the stroke of Fate concludes the number
of our pulses ; we take our leave of the *Sun*
and *Moon,* and lay our Heads in *Ashes.* The
vital flame goes out, the *Soul* retires into
another world, and the *body* to dwell in
darkness. Nor doth the last scene yield us
any more satisfaction in our *autography;* for
we are as ignorant how the Soul leaves the
light, as how it first came into it ; we know

as little how the *union* is *dissolved*, that is the chain of the so differing *subsistencies* that compound us, as how it first *commenced.* This then is the proud creature that so highly pretends to *knowledge*, and that makes such a noise and bustle for *Opinions.* The instruction of *Delphos* may shame such *confidents* into *modesty:* and till we have learn't that honest *adviso*, though from *hell*, ΓΝΩΘΙ ΣΕΑΥΤΟΝ, *Confidence* is arrogance, and *Dogmatizing* unreasonable presuming. I doubt not but the opinionative resolver, thinks all these easie *Problems*, and the Theories here accounted *Mysteries*, are to him *Revelations.* But let him suspend that conclusion till he hath weigh'd the considerations hereof, which the process of our Discourse will present him with ; and if he can unty those knots, he is able to teach all humanity, and will do well to oblige man-kinde by his informations.

CHAP. IV.

Some great Instances of our Ignorance *dis-courst of,* (1) *of things within our selves. The* Nature *of the* Soul *and it's* Origine, *glanc't at and past by:* (1) *It's* union *with the* body *is unconceivable: So* (2) *is its moving the body, consider'd either in the way of* Sir K. Digby, Des-Cartes, *or* Dr. H. More, *and the* Platonists. (3) *The manner of direction of the Spirits, as un-explicable.*

BUT that I may more closely pursue the design I am engag'd on, I shall discourse some great *Instances* of our *Ignorance* in a way of more press and strict survey. And those I shall insist on are such as (1) concern the *SOUL*, both in its *common Nature*, and *particular Faculties*. Or (2) such as are drawn from the consideration of *our own*, other *organical BODIES*, and *MATTER* in the general. And (3) some *trite* and *common APPEARANCES*. Of which I discourse in order.

If certainty were anywhere to be expected

one would think it should be in the Notices of our *Souls*, which are indeed our *selves*, and whose *sentiments* we are intimately acquainted with. In things without us, ignorance is no wonder; since we cannot profound into the *hidden things* of Nature, nor see the first springs and wheeles that set the rest a going. We view but small pieces of the *Universal* Frame, and want *Phœnomena* to make intire and secure *Hypotheses*. But if *that* whereby we *know* other things, know not it self; if our Souls are strangers to things within them, which they have far greater advantages of being acquainted with than matters of external nature; I think then this first instance will be a Fair one, for the extorting a Confession of that *Ignorance* I would have acknowledg'd.

(1) I take notice then that the learned world hath been at an infinite uncertainty about the speculation of the *Souls Nature*. In which every man almost held a distinct opinion. *Plato* call'd it, only in the general, *A self-moving substance*. *Aristotle* an *Entilechie*, or, An Hee-knew-not-what. *Hesiod* and *Anaximander* compounded It of *Earth* and *Water*. *Heraclides* made It *Light*. *Zeno* the *Quintessence* of the *four*

Elements. Xenocrates and the *Ægyptians* a *Moving Number.* The *Chaldæans* a *Vertue* without *Form. Parmenides* composed It of *Earth* and *Fire. Empedocles* of *Blood. Galen* held It an *hot Complexion. Hippocrates* a *Spirit* diffused through the *body. Varro* supposed It an heated and dispersed *Aire. Thales* a Nature without rest. And *Crates* and *Decæarchus, Nothing.* Thus have the greatest Sages differ'd in the first Theory of humane Nature ; which yet perhaps is not so desperate an Inquiry, as some others that are apprehended less difficult. And possibly most have been deceived in this *Speculation,* by seeking to grasp the *Soul* in their *Imaginations;* to which gross faculty, that purer essence is unpalpable : and we might as well expect to *taste* the *Sunbeams.* Such therefore are to be minded, that the *Soul* is seen, like other things, in the *mirrour* of it's *effects* and *attributes :* But if like Children, they'l run behind the glass to catch it, their expectations will meet with nothing but *vacuity* and *emptiness.* And though a pure *intellectual* eye may have a sight of it in *reflex* discoveries ; yet if we affect a grosser touch, like *Ixion* we shall embrace a Cloud.

(2) It hath been no less a trouble to determine the Soul's *Original*, than *Nature*. Some thought It was from the beginning of the World, and one of the first things created. Others, that 'tis an extract from the universal soul of all things. Some believe It came from the *Moon*, others from the *Stars*, or vast spaces of the *Æther* above the *Planets;* some that 'tis made by *God*, some by *Angels*, and some by the *Generant*. Whether it be immediately *created* or *traduced*, hath been the great ball of contention to the Later Ages. And yet, after all the bandying attempts of resolution ; 'Tis as much a Question as ever ; and it may be will be so till it be concluded by *Immortality*. The Patrons of Traduction accuse their Adversaries of affronting the *Attributes* of *God;* and the Assertours of *Creation* impeach *Them* of violence to the *Nature* of *Things*. Either of the opinions strongly opposeth the other ; but very feebly defends *it self*. Which occasion some to think, that both are *right*, and both *mistaken; Right* in what they say against each other ; but *Mistaken* in what they plead for their respective selves. But I shall not stirr in the waters which have been already mudded by so

B

many contentious Inquiries. The great St.
Austin, and others of the grey heads of
Reverend Antiquity, have been content to sit
down here in a profest Neutrality : And I'le
not industriously endeavour to urge men to a
confession of what they freely acknowledge ;
but shall note difficulties which are not so
usually observ'd, though as unaccountable as
these.

§. 1. I T is the saying of divine *Plato*, that
Man is natures *Horison;* dividing
betwixt the upper *Hemisphere* of *immaterial
intellects*, and this lower of *Corporeity :* And
that we are a Compound of beings distant
in extreams, is as clear as Noon. But how
the purer Spirit is united to this *clod*, is a
knot too hard for our degraded intellects
to unty. What *cement* should unite *heaven*
and *earth*, light and darkness, natures of so
divers a make, of such disagreeing attributes,
which have almost nothing, but *Being*, in
common : This is a riddle, which must be
left to the coming of *Elias*. How should a
thought be united to a marble-statue, or a
sunbeam to a lump of clay ? The freezing of
the words in the air in the Northern climes,

is as conceivable, as this strange union. That this *active spark*, this σύμφυτον πνεῦμα (as the Stoicks call it) should be confined to a Prison it can so easily pervade, is of less facil apprehension, then that the light should be pent up in a box of Crystal, and kept from accompanying its source to the lower world : And to hang weights on the wings of the winde seems far more intelligible.

In the *unions*, which we understand, the extreams are reconciled by interceding participations of natures, which have somewhat of either. But *Body* and *Spirit* stand at such a distance in their essential compositions, that to suppose an uniter of a middle constitution, that should partake of some of the qualities of both, is unwarranted by any of our faculties, yea most absonous to our reasons ; since there is not any the least affinity betwixt *length, breadth* and *thickness;* and *apprehension, judgement* and *discourse :* The former of which are the most immediate results (if not essentials) of *Matter*, the latter of *Spirit.*

§. 2. SECONDLY, We can as little give an account, how the *Soul moves* the *Body*. That, that should give motion to an unwieldy *bulk*, which it self hath neither *bulk* nor *motion* ; is of as difficil an apprehension, as any mystery in nature. For though conceiving it under some phancied appearance, and pinning on it material affections, the doubt doth not so sensibly touch us ; since under such conceptions we have the advantage of our senses to befriend us with parallels ; and gross apprehenders may not think it any more strange, then that a Bullet should be moved by the rarified fire, or the clouds carryed before the invisible winds : yet if we defæcate the notion from *materiality*, and abstract *quantity*, *place*, and all kind of *corporeity* from it, and represent it to our thoughts either under the notion of the ingenious Sir *K. Digby;* as, A pure *Mind* and *Knowledge;* or, as the admir'd *Des-Cartes* expresses it, *Une chose qui pense*, as, *A thinking substance;* it will be as hard to apprehend, as that an empty wish should remove Mountains : a supposition which if realized, would relieve *Sisyphus.* Nor yet doth the ingenious hypothesis of the most excellent *Cantabrigian* Philosopher, of the *Soul's* being an *extended penetrable* substance, relieve us ; since, how that which penetrates all bodies without the least jog or obstruction, should impress a motion on any, is by his own confession alike inconceivable. Neither will its moving the Body by a *vehicle* of Spirits, avail us ; since they are Bodies too, though of a purer mould.

And to credit the unintelligibility both of this *union* and *motion*, we need no more then to consider that when we would conceive any thing which is not obvious to our senses, we have recourse to our memories the storehouse of past observations : and turning over the treasure that is there, seek for something of like kind, which hath formerly come within the notice of our outward or inward senses. So that we cannot conceive any thing, that comes not within the verge of some of these ; but either by like *experiments* which we have made, or at least by some remoter hints which we receive from them. And where such are wanting, I cannot apprehend how the thing can be conceived. If any think otherwise, let them carefully peruse their perceptions : and, if they finde a determinate intellection of the Modes of Being, which were never in the least hinted to them by their *external* or *internal* senses ; I'le believe that such can realize *Chimæra's.* But now in the cases before us there are not the least footsteps, either of such an *Union,* or *Motion,* in the whole circumference of sensible nature : And we cannot apprehend any thing beyond the evidence of our faculties.

§. 3. THIRDLY, How the *Soul directs* the *Spirits* for the motion of the Body according to the several animal exigents ; is as perplex in the Theory, as either of the former. For the *meatus,* or passages, through which those subtill emissaries are conveyed to the respective members, being so almost infinite, and each of them drawn through so many Meanders, cross turnings, and divers roads, wherein other spirits are continually a journeying ; it is wonderful, that they should exactly perform their regular destinations without losing their way in such a wilderness : neither can the wit of man tell how they are directed. For that they are carryed by the manuduction of a Rule, is evident from the constant steadyness and regularity of their motion into the parts, where their supplies are expected : But, what that regulating efficiency should be, and how managed ; is not easily determin'd. That it is performed by meer *Mechanisme*, constant experience confutes ; which assureth us, that our *spontaneous* motions are under the *Imperium* of our *will*. At least the first determination of the Spirits into such or such passages, is from the *Soul*, what ever we hold of the after conveyances ; of which likewise I think, that all the Philosophy in the world cannot make it out to be purely *Mechanical*. But yet though we gain this, that the Soul is the principle of direction, the difficulty is as formidable as ever. For unless we allow it a kinde of inward sight of the *Anatomical* frame of its own body of every *vein*, *muscle*, and *artery ;* of the exact site, and position of them, with their several windings, and secret chanels : it is as un-conceivable how it should be the *Directrix* of such intricate motions, as that a blind man should manage a game at Chess, or Marshal an Army. But this is a kinde of *knowledge*, that we are not in the least aware of : yea many times we are so far from an attention to the inward *direction* of the *Spirits*, that our employ'd mindes observe not any method in the outward performance ; even when 'tis manag'd by variety of interchangeable motions, in which a steady direction is difficult, and a miscariage easie.   Thus an Artist will play a Lesson on an Instrument without minding a stroke ; and our tongues will run divisions in a tune not missing a note, even when our thoughts are totally engaged elsewhere : which effects are to be attributed to some secret *Art* of the Soul, which to us is utterly occult, and without the ken of our Intellects.

CHAP. V.

(4) *We can give no account of the manner of* Sensation.

§. 4. **B**UT besides the *difficulties* that lye more deep, and are of a more mysterious alloy ; we are at a loss for a *scientifical* account even of our *Senses*, the most knowable of our faculties.   Our *eyes*, that see other things, see not themselves : And the foundations of knowledge are themselves unknown.   That the soul is the sole Percipient, which alone hath *animadversion* and *sense* properly so called, and that the *Body* is only the receiver and conveyer of corporeal impressions, is as certain, as Philosophy can make it. *Aristotle* himself teaceth so much in that Maxime of his Νοῦς ὁρᾷ, κὰι νοῦς ἀκόυει. And *Plato* credits this position with his suffrage ; affirming, that 'tis the *Soul* that hath *life* and *sense*, but the *body* neither. But this is so largely prosecuted by the Great *Des-Cartes*, and is a Truth that shines so clear in the Eyes of all considering men ; that to go about industriously to prove it, were to light a candle to seek the Sun : we'll therefore suppose it, as that which needs not arrest our motion ; but yet, what are the instruments of sensible perceptions and particular conveyers of outward motions to the *seat* of *sense*, is difficult : and how the pure mind can receive information from that, which is not in the least like it self, and but little resembling what it represents ; I think inexplicable. Whether *Sensation* be made by *corporal emissions* and *material* ΕΙΔΩΛΑ, or by notions imprest on the *Æthereal* matter, and carryed by the continuity thereof to the Common sense ; I'le not revive into a Dispute : The ingenuity of the latter hath already given it almost an

absolute victory over its Rival.   But suppose
which we will, there are doubts not to be
solv'd by either.   For how the soul by
mutation made in *matter* a substance of
another kind, should be excited to action ;
and how bodily alterations and motions
should concern *that* which is subject to
neither ; is a difficulty, which confidence
may sooner triumph on, then conquer.   For
body cannot act on any thing but by *motion* ;
motion cannot be received but by *quantity*
and *matter* ; the *Soul* is a stranger to such
gross *substantiality*, and ownes nothing of
these, but that it is cloathed with by our
deceived phancies ; and therefore how can
we conceive it subject to *material impressions ?* and yet the importunity of pain, and
unavoydableness of *sensations* strongly perswade, that we are *so*.

Besides, how is it, and by what *Art* doth
it read that such an *image* or stroke in
matter (whether that of her vehicle, or of
the Brain, the case is the same) signifies
such an *object ?*   Did we learn an Alphabet
in our *Embryo*-state ?   And how comes it to
pass, that we are not aware of any such
congenite apprehensions ?   *We know what
we know ;* but do we *know* any more ?   That

by diversity of *motions* we should spell out *figures*, *distances*, *magnitudes*, *colours*, things not resembled by them ; we must attribute to some *secret deduction*. But what this *deduction* should be, or by what *mediums* this Knowledge is advanc'd ; is as dark, as Ignorance. One, that hath not the knowledge of Letters, may see the *Figures;* but comprehends not the meaning included in them : An infant may hear the sounds, and see the motion of the lips ; but hath no conception conveyed by them, no knowing what they are intended to signifie. So our *Souls*, though they might have perceived the *motions* and *images* themselves by *simple sense;* yet without some *implicit inference* it seems inconceivable, how by that means they should apprehend their *Archetypes*.

Moreover, *Images* and *Motions* are in the Brain in a very inconsiderable latitude of space, and yet they represent the greatest *magnitudes*. The image of an *Hemisphere* of the upper Globe cannot be of a wider circumference, then a Wall-nut : And how can such petty impressions notifie such vastly expanded objects, but through some kind of *Scientifical* method, and *Geometry* in the Principle ? without this it is not conceivable how *distances* should be perceiv'd, but all objects would appear in a cluster, and lye in as narrow a room as their images take up in our scanter *Craniums*. Nor will the Philosophy of the most ingenious *Des-Cartes* help us out : For, *The striking of divers filaments of the brain*, cannot well be supposed to represent *Distances*, except some such kind of *Inference* be allotted us in our faculties : the concession of which will only steed us as a Refuge for *Ignorance :* where we shall meet, what we would seem to shun.

CHAP. VI.

The nature of the Memory *unaccountable.* *'Tis consider'd particularly according to the* Aristotelian, Cartesian, Digbæan *and* Hobbian *Hypothesis.*

§. 5. THE *Memory* also is a faculty whose nature is as obscure, and hath as much of Riddle in it as any of the former : It seems to be an *Organical* Power, because bodily distempers often mar its *Idea's*, and cause a total oblivion : But what instruments the Soul useth in her review of past impressions, is a question which may drive Enquiry to despair. There are four principal *Hypotheses* by which a Resolution hath been attempted.

The *Peripatetick*, the *Cartesian*, the *Digbæan*, and the *Hobbian.* We'l examine these Accounts of the *Magnale.* And I begin with that which will needs have it self believed the most venerable for *Antiquity* and *Worth*.

(1) Then according to *Aristotle* and his *Peripatum*, Objects are conserved in the *Memory* by certain *intentional* Species, Beings, which have nothing of Matter in their Essential Constitution, but yet have a necessary subjective dependence on it, whence they are called *Material.* To this briefly.

Besides that these Species are made a *Medium* between *Body* and *Spirit*, and therefore partake of no more of Being, then what the charity of our Imaginations affords them ; and that the supposition infers a creative *energie* in the object their producent, which Philosophy allows not to Creature-Efficients ; I say, beside these, it is quite against their nature to subsist, but in the

presence and under the actual influence of
their cause; as being produc'd by an *Ema-
native Causality*, the Effects whereof dye in
the removal of their Origine.   But this
superannuated conceit deserves no more of
our remembrance, then it contributes to the
apprehension of it.   And therefore I pass on
to the *Cartesian* which speaks thus :

The *Glandula Pinealis*, in this Philosophy
made the seat of Common Sense, doth by its
motion impel the Spirits into divers parts of
the Brain; till it find those wherein are some
tracks of the object we would remember ;
which consists in this, *viz.* That the Pores of
the Brain, through the which the Spirits before
took their course, are more easily opened to
the Spirits which demand re-entrance; so
that finding those pores, they make their way
through them sooner then through others :
whence there ariseth a special motion in the
Glandula, which signifies this to be the
object we would *remember.*

But I fear there is no security neither in
this *Hypothesis*; For if *Memory* be made by
the *easie motion* of the *Spirits* through the
opened *passages*, according to what hath been
noted from *Des-Chartes* ; whence have we a
distinct Remembrance of such diversity of

Objects, whose Images without doubt pass through the same *apertures?* And how should we recal the distances of Bodies which lye in a line? Or, is it not likely, that the impell'd Spirits might light upon other Pores accommodated to their purpose, by the *Motion* of other Bodies through them? Yea, in such a *pervious* substance as the *Brain,* they might finde an easie either entrance, or *exit,* almost everywhere ; and therefore to shake every grain of corn through the same holes of a Sieve in repeated winnowings, is as easie to be performed, as this to be perceived. Besides, it's difficult to apprehend, but that these *avennues* should in a short time be stopped up by the pressure of other parts of the matter, through its natural *gravity,* or other alterations made in the *Brain:* And the opening of other *vicine passages* might quickly obliterate any tracks of these; as the making of one hole in the yielding *mud,* defaces the print of another near it; at least the accession of enlargement, which was derived from such transitions, would be as soon lost, as made.

We are still to seek then for an *Oedipus* for the Riddle ; wherefore we turn our eyes to the *Digbæan* Account, of which this is the summe ; That things are reserved in the *Memory* by some corporeal *exuviæ* and material Images; which having impinged on the Common sense, rebound thence into some vacant cells of the Brain, where they keep their ranks and postures in the same order that they entred, till they are again stirr'd up; and then they slide through the *Fancy*, as when they were first presented.

But, how is it imaginable, that those active *particles* which have no *cement* to unite them, nothing to keep them in the order they were set, yea, which are ever and anon justled by the occursion of other bodies, whereof there is an infinite store in this Repository, should so orderly keep their *Cells* without any alteration of their site or posture, which at first was allotted them? And how is it conceivable, but that carelesly turning over the *Idea's* of our mind to recover something we would remember, we should put all the other Images into a disorderly floating, and so raise a little *Chaos* of confusion, where Nature requires the exactest order. According to this account, I cannot see, but that our *Memories* would be more confused then our Mid-night compositions : For is it likely, that the divided *Atomes* which presented themselves together, should keep the same ranks in such a variety of tumultuary agitations, as happen in that liquid *Medium?* An heap of Ants on an Hillock will more easily be kept to an uniformity in motion; and the little bodies which are incessantly playing up and down the Air in their careless postures, are as capable of Regularity as these.

The last Account of the *Faculty* we are inquiring of is the *Hobbian*, according to which *Hypothesis* ; *Memory* is nothing else but the knowledge of *decaying Sense*, made by the *reaction* of one *body* against another ; or, as the Author expresses it in his *Humane Nature, A missing of Parts in an Object.* The foundation of which *Principle* (as of many of its fellows) is totally evers't by the most ingenious *Commentator* upon *Immaterial Beings*, Dr. *H. More* in his book *Of Immortality.* I shall therefore leave that cause in the hands of that most learned undertaker, and only observe two things to my present purpose. (1) Neither the *Brain*, nor *Spirits*, nor any other material substance within the *Head* can for any considerable space of time conserve *motion*. The former is of such a clammy consistence, that it can

C

no more retain it then a *Quagmire* : And
the *spirits* for their liquidity are more un-
capable than the fluid *Medium*, which is the
conveyer of *Sounds*, to persevere in the
continued repetition of *vocal Ayres.* And if
there were any other substance within us, as
fitly temper'd to preserve *motion*, as the
Author of the opinion could desire : Yet (2)
which will equally press against either of the
former, this motion would be quickly
deadned by *counter-motions;* and we should
not *remember* any thing, but till the next
impression. Much less can this *Principle*
give an account, how such an abundance of
motions should orderly succeed one another,
as things do in our *memories* : And to
remember a *song* or *tune*, it will be required, that our Souls be an *Harmony* more
then in a *Metaphor*, continually running
over in a silent whisper those *Musical accents*
which our retentive faculty is preserver of.
Which could we suppose in a single Instance ; yet a multitude of *Musical Conson-
ancies* would be as impossible, as to play a
thousand tunes on a *Lute* at once. One
motion would cross and destroy another ;
all would be clashing and discord : And the
Musicians Soul would be the most *dishar-*

monious : For, according to the tenour of
this opinion, our *memories* will be stored
with infinite variety of divers, yea contrary
motions, which must needs interfere, thwart,
and obstruct one another : and there would
be nothing within us, but *Ataxy* and disorder.

§. 6. MUCH more might be added of
the difficulties, which occur
concerning the *Understanding, Phancy, Will,*
and *Affections.* But the Controversies here-
about, are so hotly manag'd by the divided
Schools, and so voluminously everywhere
handled ; that it will be thought better to
say nothing of them, then a little. The sole
difficulties about the *Will,* its *nature,* and
sequency to the *Understanding,* &c. have
almost quite baffled inquiry, and shewn us
little else, but that our *Understandings* are
as *blind* as *it* is. And the grand question
depending hereon, Πόθεν τὸ κακόν ; I think
will not be ended, but by the final abolition
of its object. They, that would lose their
Knowledge here, let them diligently inquire
after it. Search will discover that *Ignorance,*
which is as invincible, as its Cause. These
Controversies, like some *Rivers,* the further

they run, the more they are hid. And it may be a poorer account is given to them now, then some *Centuries* past, when they were a subject of debate to the pious *Fathers.*

CHAP. VII.

How our Bodies *are* form'd *unexplicable. The* Plastick *signifies nothing* : *the* Formation *of* Plants, *and* Animals *unknown, in their Principle.* Mechanisme *solves it not. A new way propounded, which also fails of satisfaction.* (2.) *No account is yet given how the parts of* Matter *are* united. *Some consideration on* Des-Cartes *his Hypothesis, it fails of Solution.* (3.) *The Question is unanswerable, whether* Matter *be compounded of* Divisibles, *or* Indivisibles.

BUT from these I pass to the *Second* General, the consideration of *Bodies,* our own and others. For *our* own, though we *see,* and *feel,* and continually converse with them ; yet their constitution, and inward frame is an *America,* a yet undiscovered *Region.* And the saying of the Kingly Prophet, *I am wonderfully made,* may well be understood of that *admiration,* which is the *Daughter of Ignorance.* Three things I'le subjoyn concerning this *Sensible matter,* the other part of our composition.

§. 1. THAT our *Bodie's* are made according to the most curious *Artifice,* and orderly contrivance, cannot be denyed even by them, who are least beholden to *Nature.* The elegance of this composure, sav'd *Galen* from *Atheism.* And I cannot think that the branded *Epicurus, Lucretius,* and their fellows were in earnest, when they resolv'd this composition into a *fortuitous range* of *Atoms.* To suppose a *Watch,* or any other the most curious *Automaton* by the blind hits of *Chance,* to perform diversity of orderly *motions,* to shew the *hour, day* of the *Month, Tides, age* of the *Moon,* and the like, with an unparallel'd exactness, and all without the regulation of Art ; this were the more pardonable absurdity. And that this admirable *Engine* of our Bodies, whose functions are carryed on by such a multitude of *parts,* and *motions,* which neither interfere, nor impede one another in their operations; but by an *harmonious Sympathy* promote the perfection and good of the whole : That this should be an undesigned effect, is an assertion, that is more then *Melancholics Hyperbole.* I say therefore, that if we do but consider this *Fabrick* with free and unpossest mindes ; we shall easily grant, that it was some skilful *Archeus* who delineated those comely *proportions*, and hath exprest such exactly *Geometrical elegancies* in its compositions. But what this hidden *Architect* should be, and by what *instruments* and art this frame is erected ; is as *unknown* to us, as the thoughts of our cradles. The *Plastick* faculty is a fine word, and will do well in the mouth of a puzled *Emperick* : But what it is, how it works, and whose it is, we cannot learn ; no, not by a return into the *Womb* ; neither will the *Platonick* Principles unriddle the doubt : For though the Soul be supposed to be the Bodies *Maker*, and the builder of its own house ; yet by what kind of *Knowledge*, *Method*, or *Means*, is unknown : and that we should have a *knowledge* which we know not of, is an assertion which hath no commission from our Faculties. The Great *Des-Cartes* will allow it to be no better, then a downright absurdity. But yet should we suppose it, it would be evidence enough of what we aim at.

§. 2. NOR is the composition of our *own Bodies* the only wonder : we are as much nonplust by the most contemptible *Worm*, and *Plant*, we tread on. How is a drop of Dew organiz'd into an Insect ? or, a lump of Clay into a more perfect *Animal ?* How are the Glories of the Field spun, and by what Pencil are they limn'd in their un-affected bravery ?   By whose direction is the nutriment so regularly distributed unto the respective parts, and how are they kept to their specifick uniformities ? If we attempt *Mechanical* solutions, we shall never give an account, why the *Wood-cock* doth not sometimes borrow colours of the *Mag-pye;* why the *Lilly* doth not exchange with the *Daysie* ; or why it is not sometime painted with a blush of the *Rose ?*   Can *unguided matter* keep it self to such exact conform-ities, as not in the least spot to vary from the *species ?*   That divers Limners at a distance without either copy, or designe should draw the same *Picture* to an undis-tinguishable exactness, both in *form, colour,* and *features* ; is more conceivable, then that *matter*, which is so diversified both in *quantity*, *quality*, *motion*, *site*, and infinite other circumstances, should frame it self so unerringly according to the *Idea* of its kind. And though the fury of that *Apelles*, who threw his Pencil in rage upon the Picture he had essayed to draw, once casually effected those lively representations, which his Art could not describe ; yet 'tis not likely, that one of a thousand such *præcipitancies* should be crowned with so an unexpected an issue.   For though *blind matter* might reach some *elegancies* in individual effects ; yet *specifick conformities* can be no *unadvised* productions, but in greatest likelyhood, are regulated by the immediate efficiency of some *knowing* agent : which whether it be *seminal Formes*, according to the *Platonical* Principles, or whatever else we please to suppose ; the manner of its working is to us *unknown* : or if these effects are meerly *Mechanical* ; yet to learn the method of such operations may, and hath indeed been, ingeniously attempted ; but I think cannot be performed to the satisfaction of severer examination.

That all bodies both *Animal, Vegetable*

and *Inanimate*, are form'd out of such particles of matter, which by reason of their figures, will not cohære or lye together, but in such an order as is necessary to such a specifical formation, and that therein they naturally of themselves concurre, and reside, is a pretty conceit, and there are *experiments* that credit it. If after a decoction of *hearbs* in a Winter-night, we expose the liquor to the frigid air ; we may observe in the morning under a crust of Ice, the perfect appearance both in *figure*, and *colour*, of the *Plants* that were taken from it. But if we break the *aqueous Crystal*, those pretty *images* dis-appear and are presently dissolved.

Now these *airy Vegetables* are presumed to have been made, by the reliques of these *plantal emissions* whose avolation was prevented by the *condensed inclosure*. And therefore playing up and down for a while within their liquid prison, they at last settle together in their natural order, and the *Atomes* of each part finding out their proper place, at length rest in their methodical Situation ; till by breaking the *Ice* they are disturbed, and those counterfeit *compositions* are scattered into their first *Indivisibles*.

This *Hypothesis* may yet seem to receive further confirmation, from the artificial *resurrection* of *Plants* from their *ashes*, which *Chymists* are so well acquainted with : And besides, that *Salt* disolved upon fixation, returns to its affected *cubes*, the regular figures of *Minerals*, as the *Hexagonal* of *Crystal*, the *Hemi-sphærical* of the *Fairystone*, the *stellar figure* of the stone *Asteria*, and such like, seem to look with probability upon this way of formation. And I must needs say 'tis handsomly conjectur'd. But yet what those figures are, that should be thus mechanically adapted, to fall so unerringly into regular compositions, is beyond our faculties to conceive or determine. And now those *heterogenous atomes* (for such their figures are supposed) should by themselves hit so exactly into their proper residence in the midst of such tumultuary motions, cross thwartings, and *arietations* of other particles, especially when for one way of hitting right, there are thousands of missing ; there's no *Hypothesis* yet extant can resolve us. And yet had heaven afforded that miracle of men, the Illustrious *Des-Cartes* a longer day on earth, we might have expected the utmost of what ingenuity could perform herein : but his immature Fate hath unhappily disappointed us ; and prevented the most desirable Complement of his not to be equall'd *Philosophy*.

§. 3. (2) IT'S no less difficult to give an account, how the *Parts* of *Matter* and *Bodies* are *united* : For though superficial Enquirers may easily satisfie themselves by answering, that it is done by *muscles, nerves*, and other like *strings*, and *ligaments*, which Nature hath destin'd to that office ; yet, if we seek for an account how the parts of these do cohere, we shall find our selves lost in the enquiry. Nothing with any shew of success hath yet appeared on the *Philosophick Stage*, but the opinion of *Des-Cartes* ; that the Parts of *Matter* are *united* by Rest. Neither can I conceive, how any thing can be substituted in its room, more congruous to reason ; since *Rest* is most opposite to *Motion*, the immediate cause of *disunion*. But yet I cannot see, how this can account for the almost *in-dissolvible coherence* of some bodies, and the *fragility* and *solubility* of others : For if the *Union* of the *Parts* consist only in *Rest* ; it would seem, that a bagg of *dust* would be

of as firm a consistence as that of *Marble*
or *Adamant* : a Bar of *Iron* will be as easily
broken as a *Tobacco-pipe* ; and *Bajazets*
Cage had been but a sorry *Prison.* The
Ægyptian Pyramids would have been sooner
lost, then the Names of them that built
them ; and as easily blown away, as those
inverst ones of *smoke.* Nor can it be pretended for a difference, that the parts of
solid bodies are held together by *hooks*, and
angulous involutions ; since the *coherence* of
the parts of these will be of as difficult a
conception, as the former : And we must
either suppose an infinite of them holding
together on one another ; or at last come
to *parts*, that are *united* by a meer *juxta-
position*: Yea, could we suppose the former,
yet the coherence of these, would be like
the hanging together of an infinite such
of *Dust*: which *Hypothesis* would spoil the
Proverb, and *a rope of sand*, should be no
more a phrase for *Labour in vain* : For
unless there be something, upon which all
the rest may depend for their *cohesion* ; the
hanging of one by another, will signifie no
more then the mutual dependence of *causes*
and *effects* in an *infinite Series*, without a
First: the admission of which, *Atheism*

would applaud. But yet to do the *Master* of *Mechanicks* right ; somewhat of more validity in the behalf of this *Hypothesis* may be assign'd : Which is, that the closeness and compactness of the *Parts resting* together, doth much confer to the strength of the *union* : For *every thing continues in the condition, wherein it is, except something more powerful alter it* : And therefore the *parts*, that *rest* close together, must continue in the same relation to each other, till some other *body* by *motion* disjoyn them. Now then, the more *parts*, there are pen't together, the more able they will be for *resistence* ; and what hath less *compactness*, and by consequence fewer *parts*, according to the *laws* of *motion* will not be able to effect any *alteration* in it. According to what is here presented, what is most *dense*, and least *porous*, will be most *coherent*, and least *discerpible*. And if this help not, I cannot apprehend what can give an account of the former instances. And yet even this is confuted by experience ; since the most *porous spongie bodies* are oft-times the most *tough* in consistence. 'Tis easier to break a tube of *Glass* or *Crystal*, then of *Elm* or *Ash* : And yet as the *parts* of the former are more, so they are more at *rest*; since the *liquid juyce*, which is diffused through the *parts* of the *Wood*, is in a continual agitation, which in *Des-Cartes* his *Philosophy* is the cause of *fluidity*; and a proportion'd *humidity* confer's much to *union* (Sir *K. Digby* makes it the *Cement* it self); *A dry stick* will be easily broken, when *a green one* will maintain a strong resistence: and yet in the *moist* substance there is less *rest*, then in what is *dryer* and more *fragill*. Much more might be added: But I'le content my self with what's mentioned; and, not-withstanding what hath been said, I judge this account of that *miraculous wit* to be the most *ingenious* and *rational*, that *hath* or (it may be) *can* be given. I shall not therefore conclude it false; though I think the emergent *difficulties*, which are its attendants, *unanswerable*: proof enough of the weakness of our *now Reasons*, which are driven to such straights and puzzles even in things which are most *obvious*, and have so much the advantage of our *faculties*.

§. 4. (3.) THE *composition* of *Bodies*, whether it be of *Divisibles* or *Indivisibles*, is a question which must be rank'd with the *Indissolvibles*: For though it hath been attempted by the most illustrious *Wit* of all *Philosophick* Ages; yet they have done little else, but shewn their own *divisions* to be almost as *infinite*, as some suppose those of their Subject. And notwithstanding all their shifts, subtilties, newly invented Words and Modes, sly subterfuges, and studyed evasions; yet the product of all their endeavours, is but as the birth of the labouring *Mountains*, *Wind*, and *Emptiness*. Do what they can; *Actual Infinite extension everywhere*, *Equality of all bodies*, *Impossibility of Motion*, and a world more of the most palpable absurdities will press the assertors of *infinite divisibility*. Neither can it be avoided, but that all *motions* would be *equal* in *velocity*; the *lines* drawn from side to side in a *Pyramid*, may have more parts then the *Basis*, all bodies would be swallow'd up in a *point* and endless more inconsistences, will be as necessarily consequential to the opinion of *Indivisibles*. But intending only to instance in difficulties, which are not so much taken notice of; I shall refer the Reader, that would see more of this, to *Oviedo, Pontius, Ariaga, Carelton,* and other

Jesuites: whose management of this subject with equal force on either side, is a strong presumption of what we drive at.

CHAP. VIII.

Difficulties about the Motion of a Wheel, *which admit of no Solution.*

BESIDES the already mention'd difficulties, even the most ordinary trivial *occurrents*, if we contemplate them in the *Theory*, will as much puzzle us, as any of the former. Under this head I'le add three things concerning the Motion of a *Wheel*, and conclude this branch of my subject.

§. 1. FIRST then in the abstract consideration, it seems impossible that a *wheel* should *move*: I mean not the *progressive*, but that Motion which is meerly on its own *Centre*. And were it not for the information of Experience, it's most likely that *Philosophy* had long ago concluded it *impossible*: For let's suppose the wheel to be divided according to the *Alphabet*. In motion then there is a change of place, and in the motion of a *wheele* there is a succession of one part to another in the same place ; so that it seems unconceivable that *A.* should move until *B.* hath left his place : For *A.* cannot move, but it must acquire some place or other. It can acquire none but what was *B's,* which we suppose to be most immediate to it. The same space cannot contain them both. And therefore *B.* must leave its place, before *A.* can have it ; Yea, and the nature of succession requires it. But now *B.* cannot move, but into the place of *C;* and *C.* must be out, before *B.* can come in : so that the motion of *C.* will be pre-required likewise to the motion of *A*; and so onward till it comes to *Z.* Upon the same accounts *Z.* will not be able to move, till *A.* moves, being the part next to it : neither will *A.* be able to move (as hath been shewn) till *Z.* hath. And so the motion of every part will be pre-requir'd to itself. Neither can one evade, by saying, that all the parts move at once. For (1.) we cannot conceive in a *succession* but that something should be first, and that motion should begin somewhere. (2.) If the parts may all change places with one another at the same time without any respect of *priority* and *posteriority* to each

D

others *motion* :   why then may not a com-
pany of *Bullets* closely crowded together in a
Box, as well move together by a like mutual
and simultaneous exchange ? Doubtless the
reason of this ineptitude to motion in this
position is, that they cannot give way one to
another, and motion can no where begin
because of the *plenitude*.   The case is just
the same in the instance before us; and therefore we need go no further for an evidence of
its *inconceivableness*.   But yet to give it one
touch more according to the *Peripatetick*
niceness, which sayes, that one part enters in
the same *instant* that the other goes out; I'le
add this in brief : In the instant that *B.*
leaves its place, it's in it, or not :   If so ; then
A. cannot be in it in the same *instant* without a *penetration*.   If not ; then it cannot be
said to leave it in that *instant*, but to have
left it before.   These difficulties, which pinch
so in this obvious experiment, stand in their
full force against all Motion on the *Hypothesis* of *absolute plenitude*.   Nor yet have the
Defenders hereof need to take notice of them,
because they equally press a most sensible
Truth.   Neither is it fair, that the opposite
opinion of *interspers'd vacuities* should be
rejected as absurd upon the account of some

inextricable perplexities which attend it. Therefore let them both have fair play; and whichsoever doth with most ease and congruity solve the *Phenomena*, that shall have my vote for the most *Philosophick Hypothesis*.

§. 2. IT'S a difficulty no less desperate then the former, that the *parts vicine* to the *centre*, which it may be pass not over the hundredth part of *space* which those do of the extreme *circumference*, should describe their *narrower circle* but in equal time with those other, that trace so great a *round*. If they move but in the same degree of *Velocity* ; here is then an *equality in time* and *motion*, and yet a vast *inequality* in the *acquired space*. A thing which seems flatly impossible : For is it conceivable, that of two bodies setting forth together, and continuing their motion in the same swiftness, the one should so far out-go its fellow, as to move ten mile an hour, while the other moves but a furlong ? If so, 'twill be no wonder, that *the race is not to the swift*, and the *furthest way about* may well be the *nearest way home*. There is but one way that can be attempted to

D 2

untie this knot ; which is, by saying, that
the *remoter* and more out-side parts move
more swiftly than the *central* ones.   But
this likewise is as unconceivable as what
it would avoid : For suppose a right *line*
drawn from the *centre* to the *circumference,*
and it cannot be apprehended, but that the
line should be inflected, if some parts of
it move faster than others. I say if we do
abstractedly from experience contemplate
it in the *theory,* it is hard to conceive, but
that one part moving, while the other rests,
or at least moves slower (which is as rest
to a swifter motion) should change its
distance from it, and the respect, which it
had to it ; which one would think should
cause an incurvation in the *line.*

§. 3. LET there be two *Wheels* fixt on the
same Axel in *Diameter* ten inches
a piece.   Between them let there be a *little
wheel,* of two inches Diameter, fixed on the
same Axel.   Let them be moved together
on a plane, the great ones on the ground
suppose, and the little one on a Table (for
because of its parvitude it cannot reach to
the same floor with them) And you'l find
that the little wheel will move over the

same space in equal time, with equal *circulations*, with the great ones, and describe as long a line. Now this seems bigg of repugnancies, though Sense it self suffragate to its truth : For since every part of the greater wheels make a proportionable part of the line, as do the parts of the little one, and the parts of those so much exceeding in multitude the parts of this : It will seem necessary that the line made by the greater wheels should have as many parts more then the line made by the less, as the wheels themselves have in *circumference*, and so the line would be as much longer as the wheels are bigger : so that one of these absurdities seems unavoidable, either that more parts of the greater wheels go to the making one part of their lines, which will infer a *penetration* of *dimensions* ; or that the little wheel hath as many parts as the great ones, though five times in *Diameter* exceeded by them, since the lines they describe are of equal length ; or the less wheel's line will have fewer parts then the others, though of equal extent with them, since it can have no more parts then the *less circle*, nor *they* fewer then the *greater*. What offers have been made towards the resolving this difficulty, by the ingenious _Tacquett_ and others, and with what success; will be considered in the Appendix; to which, that I may pursue other matters, I remit the Inquisitive Reader.

Should I have enlarged on this Subject to the taking in of all things that claim a share in't, it may be few things would have been left unspoken to, but the _Creed_. Philosophy would not have engross'd our Pen, but we must have been forced to anger the _Intelligences_ of higher Orbs. But intending only a glance at this rugged Theam, I shall forbear to insist more on it, though the consideration of the Mysteries of _Motion_, _Gravity_, _Light_, _Colours_, _Vision_, _Sound_, and infinite such like (things _obvious_, yet _unknown_) might have been plentiful subject. I come now to trace some of the _causes_ of our _Ignorance_ and Intellectual _weakness_: and among so many it's almost as great a wonder as any of the former; that we can _say, we know_.

CHAP. IX.

Mens backwardness to acknowledge their own Ignorance and Error, though ready to find them in others. The (1) cause of the Shortness of our Knowledge, viz. the depth of Verity discours't of, as of its admixtion in Mens Opinions with false-hood, and the connexion of truths, and their mutual dependence : A second Reason of the shortness of our Knowledge, viz. because we can perceive nothing but by proportion to our Senses.

THE Disease of our *Intellectuals* is too great, not to be its own evidence : And they that feel it not, are not less *sick*, but stupidly *so*. The weakness of humane under-standing, all will confess : yet the confidence of most in their own reasonings, practically disowns it : And 'tis easier to perswade them it from others lapses then their own ; so that while all complain of our *Ignorance* and *Error*, every one exempts himself. It is acknowledged by *all*, while *every* one denies it. If the foregoing part of this Discourse, have not universally concluded our weakness : I have one Item more of mine. If knowledge can be found in the Particulars mentioned ; I must lose that, which I thought I had, *That there is none.* But however, though some should pick a quarrel with the instances I alleadged ; yet the conclusion must be owned in others. And therefore beside the general reason I gave of our intellectual disabilities, The *Fall* ; it will be worth our labour to descend to a more particular account : since it is a good degree of *Knowledge* to be acquainted with the *causes* of our *Ignorance.* And what we have to say under this head, will equally concern our *misapprehensions* and *Errors.* And the particulars I intend are *Causes* and *Evidences* of both.

§. I. (1) THEN we owe much of our *Ignorance* to the *depth* of *Knowledge* ; which is not the acquist of *superficials* and *supine* enquirers. *Democritus* his Well hath a Βάθος, and Truth floats not. The useless froth swims on the surface ; but the Pearl lies cover'd with a mass of Waters. *Verisimilitude* and *Opinion* are an easie purchase : But true *Knowledge* is *dear* and *difficult.* Like a *point* or *line*, it requires an acuteness and intention to its discovery ; while *verisimility*, like the expanded *superficies*, is an obvious sensible, and affords a large and easie field for loose inquiry. And 'tis the more difficult to find out Truth, because it is in such inconsiderable proportions scattered in a mass of *opinionative uncertainties* ; like the Silver in *Hiero's* Crown of Gold : And it is no easie piece of *Chymistry* to reduce these *Minutes* to their *unmixed selves.* The Elements are no where pure in these lower *Regions* ; and if there is any free from the admixtion of another, sure 'tis above the *concave* of the *Moon* : Neither can any boast a *knowledge* depurate from the defilement of a contrary, within this *Atmosphear* of flesh ; it dwels no where in unblended proportions, on this side the *Empyreum.* All Opinions have their *Truth*, and all have what is not *so* ; and to say *all* are *true* and *none*, is no absurdity. So that to crown our selfs with sparks, which are almost lost in such a world of *heterogeneous* natures, is as difficult as desirable. Besides, *Truth* is never *single*; to know one will require the knowledge of many. They hang together in a chain of mutual dependence ; you cannot draw one linke without attracting others. Such an Harmony cannot commence from a single string ; diversity of strokes makes it. The beauty of a Face is not known by the *Eye*, or *Nose* ; it consists in a *symmetry*, and 'tis the comparative faculty which votes it : Thus is Truth *relative*, and little considerable can be obtained by *catches*. The Painter cannot transcribe a face upon a Transient view ; it requires the information of a fixt and observant Eye : And before we can reach an exact sight of Truth's uniform perfections, this *fleeting Transitory* our *Life*, is gone. So that we see the face of Truth, but as we do one anothers, when we walk the streets, in a careless *Pass-by* ; And the most diligent observers, view but the back-side o' th' *Hangings* ; the right one is on the other side the *Grave* : And our Knowledge is but like those *broken ends* ; at best a most confused *adumbration*. Nature, that was veil'd to *Aristotle*, hath not yet uncover'd, in almost two thousand years. What he sought on the other side of *Euripus*, we must not look for on this side *Immortality*. In *easie* disquisitions we are often left to the uncertainty of a guess : yea after we have triumph'd in a supposed Εὕρηκα ; a new-sprung difficulty marrs our *Ovations*, and exposeth us to the Torment of a disappoint-ment : so that even the great *Master* of *Dogmatists* himself concludes the Scene with an *Anxius vixi, Dubius morior.*

§. 2. ANOTHER reason of our *Ignor-ance* and the *narrowness* of our *apprehensions* is ; That we cannot perceive the manner of any of Natures operations, but by proportion to our *senses*, and return to *material phantasms.* A blind man conceives not *colours*, but under the notion of some other *sensible* ; and more perfect appre-henders as grosly misconceive *Immaterials* : Our imaginations painting *Souls* and *Angels* in as little agreeing a resemblace. And had there not been any *night, shadow*, or *opacity* ; we should never have had any determinate conceit of *Darkness* ; *That* would have been as inconceivable to us, as its contrary is to him that never saw it.

But now our *senses* being scant and limited, and Natures operations subtil and various ; they must needs transcend, and out-run our faculties. They are only Natures grosser wayes of working, which are *sensible* ;

Her finer threads are out of the reach of our dull *Percipient*. Yea questionless she hath many hidden *Energies*, no wayes imitated in her obvious pieces: and therefore it is no wonder that we are so often at a loss; an infirmity beyond prevention, except we could step by step follow the tracks and Methods of *Infinite Wisdom*, which cannot be done but by him that owns it.

CHAP. X.

A third reason of our Ignorance *and* Error, viz. *the impostures and deceits of our* Senses. *The way to rectifie these mis-informations propounded.* Des-Chartes *his method the only way to Science. The difficulty of exact performance.*

§. 3. ANOTHER reason is the *Imposture* and *fallacy of our Senses*, which impose not only on common Heads, who scarce at all live to the *higher Principle*; But even more refined *Mercuries*, who have the advantages of an improved reason to disabuse them, are yet frequently captivated to these deceiving Prepossessions: appealing to a Judicature both uncommissioned and unjust ; and when the clearest Truth is to be tryed by such Judges, its innocence will not secure it from the condemning award of that *unintelligent Tribunal* : For since we live the life of *Brutes*, before we grow into *Man* ; and our understandings in this their *Non-age*, being almost meerly Passive to sensible Impressions, receiving all things in an uncontroverted and promiscuous admission : It cannot be, that our knowledge should be other, then an heap of *Misconception* and *Error*, and conceits as impertinent as the *toys* we delight *in*. All this while we have no more reason, then the ΕΙΔΩΛΟΝ ΨΥΧΗΣ (as *Plotinus* calls it) amounts to. And besides this our easie submission to sophistications of *sense*, and inability to prevent the miscariages of our *Junior* Reasons ; and that which strikes the great stroke toward our after-deceptions, is the pertinacious adherence of many of these first impressions, to our advanc't Understandings. That which is early received, if in any considerable strength of *Impress*, as it were grows into our tender natures, and is therefore of difficult remove. Thus a fright in *Minority*, or an *Antipathy* then contracted, is not worn out but with its subject. And it may be more then a *Story*, that *Nero* derived much of his cruelty from the Nurse that suckled him. Now though our coming Judgements do in part undeceive us, and rectifie the grosser Errors which our unwary Sensitive hath engaged us in ; yet others are so flesht in us, that they maintain their interest upon the deceptibility of our decayed Natures, and are cherish't there, as the legitimate issues of our reasonable faculties.

Indeed *Sense* it self detects its more palpable deceits, by a counter-evidence ; and the more ordinary Impostures seldom out- live the first *Experiments.* If our *sight* re- present a Staff as crooked in the *water;* the same faculty rectifies both it, and us, in the *thinner Element.* And if a square Tower seem round at a distance ; the eye, which mistook in the circumstance of its figure, at that remove, corrects the mistake in a due approach : Yea, and befriends those who have learn'd to make the advantage of its informations, in more remote and difficil discoveries. And though his *Sense* occasion the careless *Rustick* to judge the *Sun* no bigger then a *Cheese-fat;* yet *sense* too by a frugal improvement of its evidence, grounds the *Astronomers* knowledge, that it's bigger then this *Globe* of *Earth* and *Water*.   Which it doth not only by the advantageous assistance of a *Tube*, but by less industrious experiments, shewing in what degrees Distance minorates the Object. But yet in infinite other cases, wherein *sense* can afford none, or but very little help to dis-intangle us ; our first deceptions lose no ground, but rather improve in our riper years : so that we are not weaned from our *child-hood*, till we return to our second *Infancy* ; and even our *Grav* heads out-grow not those Errors, which we have learn't before the *Alphabet*.

Thus our *Reasons* being inoculated on *Sense*, will retain a relish of the stock they grew on : And if we would endeavour after an unmixed Knowledge ; we must *unlive* our former *lives*, and (inverting the practice of *Penelope*) undo in the *day* of our more ad-vanc'd understandings, what we had spun in the *night* of our *Infant-ignorance*.   He that would rebuild a decayed *structure*, must first pluck down the former *ruines*.   A *fabrick*, though high and beautiful, if founded on *rubbish*, is easily made the triumph of the winds : And the most pompous seeming Knowledge, that's built on the unexamin'd prejudices of *Sense*, stands not, but till the *storm ariseth* ; the next strong encounter discovers its weakness, in a shameful over-throw. Since then, a great part of our scientifical *Treasure* is most likely to be *adulterate*, though all bears the image and superscription of *Truth* ; the only way to know what is sophisticate, and what is not so, is to bring all to the *Examen* of the Touchstone : For the prepossessions of *sense* having (as is shewen) so mingled themselves with our Genuine Truths, and being as plau-sible to appearance as they, we cannot gain a true assurance of any, but by suspending our assent from all, till the deserts of each, dis-cover'd by a strict enquiry, claim it. Upon this account I think the *method* of the most excellent *Des-Cartes* not unworthy its Author ; and (since *Dogmatical Ignorance* will call it so) a *Scepticism*, that's the only way to *Science*. But yet this is so difficult in the impartial and exact performance, that it may be well reckon'd among the bare *Possibi-lities*, which never commence into a *Futurity* : It requiring such a *free, sedate,* and *intent* minde, as it may be is no where found but among the *Platonical Idæa's.* Do what we can, Prejudices will creep in, and hinder our Intellectual Perfection : And though by this means we may get some comfortable allay to our distempers ; yet can it not perfectly cure us of a disease, that sticks as close to us as our Natures.

CHAP. XI.

Two Instances of Sensitive *deception.* (1) *Of the* Quiescence *of the* Earth. *Sense is the great inducement to its belief ; its testimony deserves no credit in this case, though it do move, Sense would present it as immoveable. The Sun to Sense is as much devoid of motion as the Earth. The Cases wherein motion is insensible, Applyed to the Earths motion. The unweildiness of its bulk is no argument of its immobility.*

TO Illustrate the Particular I am discoursing of, I'le indeavour to detect the unlucky influence of *Sensitive* prejudice by a double Instance ; the free debate of which I conceive to be of importance, though

E

hitherto for the most part obstructed, by the peremptory conclusion of a faculty which I shall make appear to have no suffrage in the case of either : And the pleasantness and concernment of the *Theories*, if it be one, I hope will attone the *Digression*.

§. 2. F*IRST*, it is generally opinion'd that the *Earth rests* as the Worlds *centre*, while the *Heavens* are the subject of the *Universal Motions* ; And, *as immoveable as the Earth*, is grown into the credit of being *Proverbial*. So that for a man to go about to counter-argue this belief, is as fruitless as to whistle against the windes. I shall not undertake to maintain the *Paradox*, that confronts this almost *Catholick* Opinion. Its assertion would be entertained with the hoot of the Rabble : the very mention of it as possible, is among the most ridiculous ; and they are likely most severely to judge it, who least understand what it is they censure. But yet the Patronage of as great *Wits*, as it may be e're saw the Sun, such as *Pythagoras, Des-Cartes, Copernicus, Galilæo, More, Kepler*, and generally the *vertuosi* of the awakened world, hath gain'd it a more favourable censure with learned mankind ; and advanc'd it far above either vain, or contemptible. And if it be a mistake, it's only so : There's no *Heresie* in such an harmless aberration ; at the worst, with the ingenuous, the probability of it will render it a lapse of easie Pardon.

Now whether the *Earth* move or rest, I undertake not to determine. My work is to prove, that the common inducement to the belief of its *quiescence*, the testimony of *sense*, is weak and frivolous : to the end, that if upon an unprejudiced tryal, it be found more consonant to the *Astronomical Phænomena* ; its *Motion* may be admitted, notwithstanding the seeming contrary evidence of unconcerned *Senses*. And I think what follows will evince, that this is no so absurd an *Hypothesis*, as Vulgar Philosophers acount it ; but that, though it *move*, its *motion* must needs be as *insensible*, as if it were *quiescent* ; and the assertion of it would then be as uncouth and harsh to the sons of *Sense*, that is, to the generality of Mankind, as now it is.

That there is a *motion*, which makes the vicissitudes of day and night, and constitutes the successive Seasons of the year ; *Sense*

may assure us ; or at least the comparative
Judgment of an higher faculty, made upon its
immediate evidence : But whether the *Sun*,
or *Earth*, be the common *Movent*, cannot be
determin'd but by a further appeal. If we
will take the literal evidence of our Eyes, the
Æthereal Coal moves no more then this
Inferior clod doth : For where ever in the
Firmament we see it, it's represented to us,
as fixt in that part of the enlightened
Hemisphear. And though an after account
discover, that he hath changed it's *Site* and
respect to this our *Globe*; yet whether that
were caused by its translation from us, or
ours from it, Sense leaves us in an *Ignoramus :* So that if we are resolved to stand
to its Verdict, it must be by as great a
Miracle if the *Sun* ever *move*, as it was that
it once *rested*, or what ever else was the subject of that supernal change. And if upon a
meer sensible account we will deny Motion
to the *Earth* ; upon the same inducement we
must deny it the *Sun* ; and the *Heavens*
will lose their *First Moveable.* But to draw
up closer to our main design, We may the
better conceive that, though the *Earth move*,
yet its *Motion* must needs be insensible ; if

we consider that in these cases relating to our purpose, *Motion* strikes not the *Sense.*

(1.) Then if the *Motion* be very slow, we perceive it not. We have no sense of the *accretive* motion of *Plants* or *Animals*; And the sly *shaddow* steals away upon the *Dyal*; And the quickest Eye, can discover no more but that *'tis gone.* Which *insensibility* of slow motions I think may thus be accounted for; *Motion* cannot be perceived without the perception of its *Terms, viz.* The parts of space which it immediately left, and those which it next acquires. Now the space left and acquir'd in every sensible moment in such slow progressions, is so inconsiderable, that it cannot possibly move the *sense*; (which by reason either of its constitutional dulness, or the importunity of stronger impressions, cannot take notice of such parvitudes) and therefore neither can the Motion depending thereon, be any more observable, then we find it.

2. If the *sentient* be carryed *passibus æquis* with the body, whose *motion* it would observe; (supposing that it be *regular* and *steddy*) In this case the remove is insensible, at least in its proper subject. We perceive not a Ship to move, while we are in

it ; but our sense transfers its motion to the neighbouring shores, as the Poet, *Littus campiq; recedunt.* And I question not, but if any were born and bred under Deck, and had no other information but what his sense affords ; he would without the least doubt or scruple, opinion, that the house he dwelt in, was as stable and fixt as ours. To express the reason according to the Philosophy of *Des-Cartes*, I suppose it thus : *Motion* is not perceived, but by the *successive strikings* of the object upon divers *filaments* of the *Brain* ; which diversifie the representation of its *site* and *distance.* But now when the motion of the object is common with it, to our selves; it retains the same relation to our *sense*, as if we both *rested :* For striking still on the same *strings* of the Brain, it varies not its *site* or *distance* from us ; and therefore we cannot possibly perceive its motion : nor yet upon the same account our own ; least of all, when we are carryed with-out any *conamen* and endeavour of ours, which in our particular progressions betrayes them to our notice.

Now then, The *Earths motion* (if we suppose it to have any) hath the concurrence of both, to render it *insensible* ; and therefore we need no more proof to conclude the necessity of its being so.

For though the First seems not to belong to the present case, since the supposed motion will be near a thousand miles an hour under the *Equinoctional line*; yet it will seem to have no *Velocity* to the *sense* any more than the received *motion* of the *Sun* and for the same reason. Because the distant points in the *Celestial expanse* (from a various and successive respect to which the length, and consequently the swiftness of this *motion* must be calculated) appear to the Eye in so small a degree of *elongation* from one another, as bears no proportion to what is *real*. For since the Margin of the *Visible Horizon* in the Heavenly *Globe* is Parallel with that in the Earthly, accounted but 120 miles *diameter*; Sense must needs measure the *Azimuths*, or *Vertical Circles*, by triplication of the same *diameter* of 120. So that there will be no more proportion betwixt the *sensible* and *real* celerity of the *Terrestrial Motion*, then there is between the *visible* and *rational dimension* of the celestial *Hemisphear*, which is none at all.

But if sensitive prejudice will yet confidently maintain the Impossibility of the

Hypothesis, from the supposed *unwieldiness* of its massie bulk, grounded on our experience of the ineptitude of *great* and *heavy* bodies to *Motion* : I say this is a meer Imposture of our *Senses*, the fallacy of which we may avoid, by considering ; that the *Earth* may as easily move, notwithstanding this pretended indisposition of its *magnitude*, as those much vaster *Orbs* of *Sun* and *Stars*. He that made it, could as well give motion to the whole, as to the parts ; the constant agitation of which is discover'd in natural productions : and to *both*, as well as *Rest* to either : Neither will it need the assistance of an *Intelligence* to perpetuate the begun *Rotation* : Since according to the Indispensible *Law* of *Nature* (*That every thing should continue in the state wherein it is, except something more powerful hinder it*) it must persevere in Motion, unless obstructed by a *Miracle*. Neither can *Gravity*, which makes great bodies hard of Remove, be any hinderance to the *Earths motion*: since even the *Peripatetick Maxime*, *Nihil gravitat in suo loco*, will exempt it from the indisposition of that *Quality* ; which is nothing but the tendency of its parts, which are ravish't from it, to their desired *Centre*.

And the *French Philosophy* will inform us, that the *Earth* as well as other bodies is indifferent in it self to *Rest*, or its contrary.

CHAP. XII.

Another instance of the deceptions *of our* Senses : *which is of translating the Idea of our Passions to things without us. Properly and formally heat is not in the fire, but is an expression of our sentiment. Yet in propriety of speech the Senses themselves are never deceived, but only administer an occasion of deceit to the understanding : prov'd by reason, and the Authority of St.* Austin.

SECONDLY the *Best Philosophy* (the deserved Title of the *Cartesian*) derives all *sensitive perception* from *Motion*, and corporal impress ; some account of which we have above given. Not that the Formality of it consists in *material Reaction*, as Master *Hobbs* affirms, totally excluding any immaterial concurrence : But that the representations of Objects to the Soul, the only *animadversive principle*, are conveyed by motions made upon the immediate Instruments of Sense. So that the diversity of our Sensations ariseth from the diversity of the *motion* or *figure* of the object ; which in a different manner affect the Brain, whence the Soul hath its immediate intelligence of the quality of what is presented. Thus the different effects, which *fire* and *water*, have on us, which we call *heat* and *cold*, result from the so differing *configuration* and *agitation* of their *Particles* ; and not from, I know not what *Chimerical beings*, supposed to inhere in the objects, their cause, and thence to be propagated by many petty *imaginary productions* to the seat of *Sense*. So that what we term *heat* and *cold*, and other qualities, are not properly according to *Philosophical* rigour in the Bodies, their Efficients : but are rather *Names* expressing our *passions* ; and therefore not strictly attributable to any thing without us, but by *extrinsick denominations*, as *Vision* to the Wall.

This I conceive to be an *Hypothesis*, well worthy a rational belief: and yet is it so abhorrent from the Vulgar, that they would as soon believe *Anaxagoras*, that *snow is black*, as him that should affirm, it is not *white* ; and if any should in earnest assert, that the *fire* is not formally *hot*, it would be thought that the heat of his brain had fitted him for *Anticyra*, and that his head were *so* to madness : For it is conceived to be as certain, as our faculties can make it, that the same qualities, which we resent within us, are in the object, their Source. And yet this confidence is grounded on no better foundation, then a delusory prejudice, and the vote of *misapplyed sensations*, which have no warrant to determine either one or other. I may indeed conclude, that I am formally *hot* or *cold* ; I feel it. But whether these qualities are *formally*, or only *eminently* in their producent ; is beyond the knowledge of the *sensitive*. Even the *Peripatetick Philosophy* will teach us, that *heat* is not in the Body of the *Sun*, but only *virtually*, and as in its cause ; though it be the Fountain and great Distributour of warmth to the neather Creation : and yet none urge the evidence of *sense* to disprove it : Neither can it with any more Justice be alledged against this *Hypothesis*. For if it be so as *Des-Cartes* would have it ; yet *sense* would constantly present it to us, as *Now*. We should feel heat as *constantly* from *Fire* ;

it would increase in the same degrees, in
our approach, and we should finde the same
excess within the flame : which yet I think
to be the chief inducements to the adverse
belief : For *Fire* (I retain the instance, which
yet may be applied to other cases) being
constant in its specifical motions in those
smaller derivations of it, which are its
instruments of action, and therefore in the
same manner striking the sentient, though
gradually varying according to the proportions of more or less quantity or agitation,
&c. will not fail to produce the same effect
in us, which we call *heat*, when ever we are
within the Orb of its activity.   So that the
heat must needs be augmented by prox-
imity, and most of all within the *Flame*,
because of the more *violent motion* of the
particles there, which therefore begets in us
a stronger sentiment.   Now if this *motive
Energie*, the instrument of this active
Element, must be called *Heat* ; let it be *so*,
I contend not.   I know not how otherwise to
call it :   To impose names is part of the
Peoples Charter, and I fight not with *Words*,
Only I would not that the *Idea* of our
Passions should be appli'd to any thing
without us, when it hath its subject no where

but in our selves. This is the grand deceit, which my design is to detect, and if possible, to rectifie.

We have seen then two notorious instances of *sensitive deception*, which justifie the charge of *Petron. Arbiter.*

> *Fallunt nos oculi, vagiq ; sensus*
> *Oppressâ ratione mentiuntur.*

And yet to speak properly, and to do our *senses* right, simply they are not deceived, but only administer an occasion to our forward *understandings* to deceive themselves : and so though they are some way accessory to our delusion ; yet the more principal faculties are the *Capital offenders.* If the *Senses* represent the *Earth* as *fixt* and *immoveable;* they give us the truth of their *Sentiments.* To *sense*, it is *so*, and it would be deceit to present it otherwise. For (as we have shewn) though it do *move* in it self; it *rests* to us, who are carry'd with it. And it must needs be to *sense* unalterably *quiescent*, in that our *own* Rotation prevents the variety of *successive Impress* ; which only renders motion *sensible.* And so if we erroneously attribute our particular incommunicable sensations to things, which do no more resemble them then the *effect* doth its *æquivocal cause* ; our *senses* are not in fault, but our *precipitate judgments*. We *feel* such, or such a *sentiment* within us, and herein is no cheat or misprision : 'tis truly so, and our *sense* concludes nothing of its Rise or Origine. But if hence our Understandings falsly deduct, that there is the same quality in the *external impressor* ; 'tis it is *criminal*, our *sense* is *innocent*. When the *Ear* tingles, we really hear a *sound* : If we judge it without us, it's the fallacy of our *Judgments*. The *apparitions* of our frighted *Phancies* are real *sensibles* : But if we translate them without the compass of our Brains, and apprehend them as external objects ; it's the unwary rashness of our *Understanding* deludes us. And if our disaffected Palates resent nought but bitterness from our choicest viands, we truly tast the unpleasing quality, though falsly conceive it in that, which is no more then the occasion of its production. If any find fault with the novelty of the notion ; the learned *St. Austin* stands ready to confute the charge : and they who revere *Antiquity*, will

derive satisfaction from so venerable a
suffrage. He tells us, *Si quis remum frangi
in aquâ opinatur, &, cum aufertur, integ-
rari; non malum habet internuncium, sed
malus est Judex.* And onward to this purpose, The sense could not otherwise perceive
it in the *water*, neither ought it : For since
the *Water* is one thing, and the *Air* another ;
'tis requisite and necessary, that the *sense*
should be as different as the *medium* :
Wherefore the Eye sees aright ; if there be
a mistake ; 'tis the Judgment's the Deceiver.
Elsewhere he saith, that our Eyes mis-inform
us not, but faithfully transmit their resentment to the mind. And against the
Scepticks, That it's a piece of injustice to
complain of our *senses,* and to exact from
them an account, which is beyond the sphear
of their notice : and resolutely determines,
Quicquid possunt videre oculi, verum vident.
So that what we have said of the *senses
deceptions,* is rigidly to be charg'd only on
our careless Understandings, misleading us
through the ill management of sensible
informations. But because such are commonly known by the name of the *Senses
deceipts* (somewhat the more justifiably in
that they administer the occasion) I have

thought good to retain the usual way of speaking, though somewhat varying from the manner of apprehending.

CHAP. XIII.

A fourth Reason of our Ignorance *and* Error, viz. *the fallacy of our* Imaginations ; *an account of the nature of that faculty ; Instances of its deceptions ; Spirits are not in a place ;* Intellection, Volition, Decrees, *&c. cannot properly be ascrib'd to God. It is not* Reason *that opposeth* Faith, *but* Phancy *: the interest which Imagination hath in many of our Opinions, in that it impresses a perswasion without evidence.*

FOURTHLY, we *erre* and come short of *Science,* because we are so frequently mislead by the evil conduct of our *Imaginations* ; whose irregular strength and importunity doth almost perpetually abuse us. Now to make a full and clear discovery of our *Phancies* deceptions ; 'twill be requisite to look into the nature of that *mysterious faculty.* In which survey we must trace the

Soul in the wayes of her *intellectual* actions ; whereby we may come to the distinct know-ledge of what is meant by *Imagination*, in contradistinction to some other Powers. But first premising, that the *Souls nature* (at least as far as concerns our inquiry) consists in *intelligibility* : And secondly, that when we speak of *Powers* and *Faculties* of the Soul, we intend not to assert with the *Schools*, their *real* distinction from it, or each other, but only a *modal* diversity. Therefore I shall distribute *Intellectual operations* ac-cording to the known *triple* division, though with some difference of representation.

The first is *simple apprehension*, which denotes no more, then the souls naked *Intellection* of an object, without either *composition* or *deduction*. The foundation of this act, as to materials, is *sensitive preception*. Now our *simple* apprehension of corporal objects, if *present*, we call *Sense* ; if absent, we properly name it *Imagination*. When we would conceive a *material* object, our *phancies* present us with it's *Idæa*. But in our Notion of *spirituals*, we, as much as we can, strip them of all *material Phan-tasmes* ; and thus they become the object of our *Intellects*, properly so called. All this

F

while the *soul* is, as it were, *silent*; and in a more passive way of reception.

But the *second act* advanceth propositions from *simple intellections*: and hereby we have the knowledge of the *distinctions* or *identities* of objects. Now here, as in the former, where they are purely *material*; the Judgment is made by the *Imagination*: if otherwise, we refer it to the *Understanding*.

The *third Act*, is that which connects *Propositions* and deduceth *Conclusions* from them: and *this* the Schools call *Discourse*; and we shall not miscal it, if we name it, *Reason. This* as it supposeth the two former, so is it grounded on certain *congenite propositions*; which I conceive to be the very *Essentials* of Rationality. Such are, *Quodlibet est, vel non est*; *Impossibile est idem esse, & non esse*; *Non entis nulla sunt prædicata*, and such like. Not that every one hath naturally a *formal* and *explicit* notion of these *Principles*: For the Vulgar use them, without knowledge of them, under any such *express* consideration; But yet there was never any born to *Reason* without them. Now when the conclusion is deduc'd from the unerring dictates of our faculties; we say the Inference is *Rational*: But when from mis-apprehended, or ill-compounded phantasmes ; we ascribe it to the *Imagination.* So we see, there is a triple operation of the *Phancy* as well as *Intellect* ; and these powers are only *circumstantially* different. In this method we intend a distinct, though short account, how the *Imagination* deceives us.

First then, the *Imagination*, which is of *simple* perception, doth never of it self and directly mislead us ; as is at large declared in our former discourse of *Sense.* Yet is it the almost fatal means of our deception, through the unwarrantable *compositions, divisions*, and *applications*, which it occasions the *second Act* to make of the *simple Images.* Hence we may derive the *Visions, Voyces, Revelations* of the *Enthusiast* : the strong Idea's of which, being conjur'd up into the *Imagination* by the heat of the *melancholized* brain, are judged exterior *Realities* ; when as they are but motions within the *Cranium.* Hence Story is full of the wonders, it works upon *Hypochondriacal Imaginants* ; to whom the grossest absurdities are infallible certainties, and free reason an Impostour. That *Groom*, that conceited himself an *Emperour*, thought all as irrational

as disloyal, that did not acknowledge him :
And he, that supposed himself made of
Glass, thought them all *mad*, that disbelieved him.   But we pity, or laugh at
those fatuous *Extravagants* ; while yet our
selves have a considerable dose of what
makes them *so* : and more sober heads have
a set of misconceits, which are as absurd to
an unpassionated *reason*, as those to our
unabused *senses*.   And as the greatest
counter-evidence to those distemper'd phancies is none : so in the more ordinary deceits,
in which our Imaginations insensibly engage
us, we give but little credit to the uncor-
rupted suggestions of the faculty, that should
disabuse us.

   That the *Soul* and *Angels* are devoid of
quantity and *dimension*, hath the suffrage of
the most ; and that they have nothing to
do with grosser *locality*, is as generally
opinion'd : but who is it, that retains not a
great part of the imposture, by allowing
them a *definitive Ubi*, which is still but
Imagination? He that said, a *thousand*
might dance on the *point of a Needle*,
spake but grossly ; and we may as well
suppose them to have *wings*, as a proper
Ubi.   We say, *Spirits* are where they

operate : But strictly to be in a *place*, or *ubi*, it may be is a *material* Attribute, and incompatible with so pure a Nature. We ask not, in what place a *thought* is, nor are we solicitous for the *Ubi* of *Vertue*, or any other *Immaterial* accidents. *Relations*, *Ubications*, *Duration*, the *vulgar* Philosophy admits to be *Something* ; and yet to enquire in what *place* they are, were gross and incongruous. So that, if *to be*, and *to be in a place* be not reciprocal ; I know not why *Spirits* may not be exempted, having as much to plead from the *purity* of their essence, as any thing in nature. And yet *Imagination* stands so strongly against the notion, that it cannot look for the favour of a very diffusive entertainment.

But we are more dangerously deceiv'd, when judging the *Infinite Essence* by our narrow selves ; we ascribe *Intellections*, *Volitions*, *Decrees*, *Purposes*, and such like *Immanent actions* to that nature, which hath nothing in common with us, as being infinitely above us. Now to use these as *Hypotheseis*, as himself in his Word, is pleas'd to *low* himself to our capacities, is allowable : But a strict and rigorous imputation is derogatory to him, and arro-

gant in us. To say, that *God* doth *eminently*
contain all those effects in his glorious
simple Essence, that the creature can
produce or act by such a *faculty, power,* or
affection ; is to affirm him to be what he
is, *Infinite.* Thus, to conceive that he can
do all those things in the most perfect
manner, which we do upon *understanding,*
willing, and *decreeing* ; is an apprehension
suteable to his *Idea* : But to fix on him the
formality of *faculties,* or *affections* ; is the
Imposture of our *Phancies,* and contradictory to his *Divinity.* 'Tis this deception
misleads the contending world ; and is
the Author of most of that darkness and
confusion, that is upon the face of the
Controversies of *Dort.* We being then thus
obnoxious to fallacy in our *apprehensions*
and *judgments,* and so often imposed upon
by these deceptions ; our *Inferences* and
Deductions must needs be as unwarrantable,
as our *simple* and *compound* thoughts are
deceitful. So that the *reason* of the far
greatest part of mankind, is but an aggregate
of mistaken phantasms ; and in things *not*
sensible, a constant delusion. Yea the
highest and most improved Spirits, are
frequently caught in the entanglements of

a tenacious *Imagination* ; and submit to
its obstinate, but delusory suggestions.
Thus we are involv'd in inextricable perplexities about the *Divine Nature*, and
Attributes ; and in our reasonings about
those sublimities are puzled with contradictions, which are but the toyings of our
Phancies, no absurdities to our more *defæcate*
faculties. What work do our *Imaginations*
make with *Eternity* and *Immensity* ? and
how are we gravell'd by their cutting
Dilemma's ? I'm confident many have
thus *imagin'd* themselves out of their
Religion ; and run a ground on that more
desperate absurdity, *Atheism.* To say,
Reason opposeth *Faith*, is to scandalize
both : 'Tis *Imagination* is the Rebel ;
Reason contradicts its impious suggestions.
Nor is our *Reason* any more accountable
for the Errours of our *Opinions* ; then our
holiness for the *immoralities* of our *Lives* :
And we may as well say, that the *Sun* is
the cause of the *shadow*, which is the effect
of the intercepting *opacity*, as either. *Reason*
and *Faith* are at perfect *Unisons* : The
disharmony is in the *Phancy.* Τὸ λογικόν
ἔστι θεῖον, is a saying of *Plato's* ; and well
worthy a Christian subscription, *Reason*

being the Image of the Creator's Wisdom copyed out in the Creature. Though indeed, as 'tis now in the subject, 'tis but an amassment of *imaginary conceptions, præjudices, ungrounded opinions,* and infinite Impostures ; and 'tis no wonder, if these are at odds with the Principles of our belief : But all this is but *apish Sophistry,* and to give it a Name so *Divine* and *excellent,* is abusive and unjust.

There is yet another as deplorable a deceit of our *Imaginations,* as any : which is, its impressing a strong perswasion of the Truth of an *Opinion,* where there is no evidence to support it. And if it be such, as we never heard question'd or contradicted, 'tis then unsuspected. The most of mankind is led by *opinionative* impulse, and *Imagination* is prædominant. An ungrounded *credulity* is cry'd up for *faith* ; and the more vigorous impressions of *Phancy,* for the *Spirits* motions. These are the grand delusions of our Age, and the highest evidence of the *Imaginations* deceptions. This is the *spirit,* that works in the children of *Phancy* ; and we need not seek to remoter resolutions. But the excellent Dr. *H. More* hath follow'd *Enthusiastick effects* to their proper *Origine,*

and prevented our endeavours of attempting
it. His discourse of *Enthusiasm* compleatly
makes good the Title ; and 'tis as well a
Victory, as a *Triumph*.

CHAP. XIV.

A fifth Reason, the præcipitancy *of our*
Understandings *; the reason of it. The
most close engagement of our minds requisite to the finding of truth; the difficulties of the performance of it. Two
instances of our præcipitating; as the
concluding things* impossible, *which to
Nature are not so ; and the joyning
Causes with irrelative Effects.*

§. 5.   AGAIN, another account of the
shortness of our *Reasons* and
easiness of deception, is, the *forwardness* of
our *Understandings assent*, to slightly
examin'd *conclusions*, contracting many
times a firm and obstinate belief from
weak inducements ; and that not only in
such things, as immediately concern the
sense, but in almost every thing that falls
within the scope of our enquiry. For the

declarement of this, we are to observe,
That every being uncessantly aspires to
its own *perfection*, and is restless till it
obtain it ; as is the trembling *Needle*, till
it find its *beloved North*. Now the perfection of a Faculty is Union with its
Object, to which its respective actions are
directed, as the scope and term of its endeavours. Thus our Understanding being
prefected by *Truth*, with all the impatience,
which accompanies strong desire, breaths
after its enjoyment. But now the *good*
and perfection of *being*, which every thing
reacheth at, must be *known*, and that in
the particular instances thereof ; or else
'tis not attain'd : and if it be mistaken,
that *being* courts deceit and its own
delusion. This *Knowledge* of their *Good*,
was at first as natural to all things, as the
desire on't : otherwise this innate propension
would have been as much a torment and
misery to those things that are capable
of it, as a needless impertinency to all
others. But Nature shoots not at *Rovers*.
Even *inanimates*, though they know not
their perfection themselves, yet are they
not carryed on by a blind unguided *impetus* :
But that which directs them, knows it.

The next orders of being have some sight of it themselves : And man most perfectly had it, before his unhappy defection. So then beside this general propensity to Truth, the *Understanding* must know what is *so*, before it can *assent*. The former we possess (it may be) as entirely as when Nature gave it us : but of the latter, little but the capacity : So that herein have we made our selves of all creatures the most miserable. And now, such an Infinite of *uncertain opinions*, bare *probabilities*, specious *falshoods*, spreading themselves before us, and solliciting our belief, and we being thus greedy of *Truth*, and yet so unable to discern it : it cannot be, that we should reach it any otherwise, then by the most close *meditation* and engagement of our minds ; by which we must endeavour to estrange our assent from every thing, which is not *clearly* and *distinctly* evidenc't to our *faculties*. But this is so difficult ; and as hath been intimated, so almost infeasable ; that it may well drive modesty to despair of *Science*. For though possibly Assiduity in the most fixed cogitation be no trouble or pain to *immaterializ'd spirits* ; yet is it more, then our *embodyed souls* can bear

without lassitude or distemper. For in this
terrestrial state there are few things trans-
acted, even in our *Intellectual* part, but
through the help and furtherance of *corporal*
Instruments ; which by more then ordinary
usage lose their edge and fitness for action,
and so grow inept for their respective
destinations. Upon this account our *senses*
are dull'd and spent by any extraordinary
intention ; and our very *Eyes* will ake, if
long fixt upon any difficultly discerned
object. Now though *Meditation* be to be
reckoned among the most abstracted operations of our minds ; yet can it not be performed without a considerable proportion
of *Spirits* to assist the Action, though indeed
such as are furnish't out of the bodies purer
store. Which I think to be clear from
hence, in that fixed seriousness herein, heats
the brain in some to distraction, causeth an
aking and diziness in sounder heads, hinders
the works of Nature in its lower and animal
functions, takes away or lessens pain in
distemper'd parts, and seldom leaves any
but under a wearysome dulness, and inactivity : Arguments of sufficient validity
to justifie our assent to this, that the *spirits*
are imploy'd in our most *intense* cogitations,

yea in such, whose objects are least *material.* Now the managing and carrying on of this work by the *Spirits* instrumental *co-efficiency* requires, that they be kept together without distraction or dissipation ; that so they may be ready to receive and execute the orders and commissions of the commanding faculty. If either of these happen, all miscarries : as do the works of Nature, when they want that *heat,* which is requisite for their intended *perfection.* And therefore, for the prevention of such inconveniences in *meditation,* we choose recess and solitude.

But now if we consider the *volatile* nature of those *officious Assistants,* and the several causes which occur continually, even from the meer *Mechanism* of our Bodies to scatter and disorder them, besides the excursions of our roving *phancies* (which cannot be kept to a close attendance) ; it will be found very hard to retain them in any long service, but do what we can, they'l get loose from the Minds *Regimen.* So that it's no easie matter to bring the body to be what it was intended for, the *Souls servant* ; and to confine the *imagination,* of as facil a performance, as the *Goteham's* design of hedging in the *Cuckow.* And though some constitutions

are genially disposited to this mental
seriousness ; yet they can scarce say, *Nos
numeri sumus* : yea in the most advantag'd
tempers, this disposition is but *comparative* ;
when as the most of men labour under disadvantages, which nothing can rid them of,
but that which loosens them from this mass
of flesh. Thus the boyling blood of youth,
fiercely agitating the fluid Air, hinders that
serenity and fixed stayedness, which is
necessary to so severe an intentness : And
the frigidity of decrepit age is as much its
enemy, not only through penury of *spirits*,
but by reason of its dulling moisture. And
even in the temperate *zone* of our life, there
are few bodies at such an *æquipoiz* of
humours ; but that the prevalency of some
one indisposeth the *Spirits* for a work so
difficult and serious : For *temperamentum
ad pondus*, may well be reckon'd among the
Philosophical unattainables. Besides, the
bustle of business, the avocations of our
senses, and external pleasures, and the
noyse and din of a clamorous world, are
impediments not to be master'd by feeble
endeavours. And to speak the full of my
Sentiments, I think never man could boast
it, without the Precincts of *Paradise* ; but

He, that came to gain us a better *Eden* then we lost.

So then, to direct all this to our end, the mind of man being thus naturally amorous of, and impatient for *Truth*, and yet averse to, and almost incapacitated for that diligent and painful search, which is necessary to its discovery; it must needs take up short, of what is really *so*, and please it self in the possession of imaginary appearances, which offering themselves to its embraces in the borrowed attire of that, which the *enamour'd Intellect* is in pursuit of, our impatient minds entertain these counterfeits, without the least suspicion of their cousenage. For as the *Will*, having lost its true and substantial *Good*, now courts the shadow, and greedily catches at the vain shews of *superficial* bliss : so our no less degenerate *understandings* having suffered as sad a divorce from their dearest object, are as forward to defile themselves with every meretricious semblance, that the variety of opinion presents them with. Thus we see the inconsiderate vulgar, prostrating their assent to every shallow appearance : and those, who are beholden to *Prometheus* for a finer mould, are not furnisht with so much truth as otherwise they might be owners of, did not this *precipitancy* of *concluding* prevent them : As 'tis said of the industrious *Chymist*, that by catching at it too soon, he lost the long expected treasure of the *Philosophical Elixir.* Now this precipitancy of our understandings is an occasion of a double error, very injurious to the encrease of Knowledge. To instance,

(1.) Hence we conclude many things *Impossibilities*, which yet are easie *Feasables.* For by an unadvised transiliency leaping from the effect to its remotest cause, we observe not the connexion through the interposal of more immediate causalities ; which yet at last bring the extreams together without a *Miracle.* And hereupon we hastily conclude *that impossible*, which we see not in the proximate capacity of its *Efficient.* That a single *Hair* should root up an *Oak* (which the Mathematicks teach us to be possible) by common heads will be thought an absurd and extravagant expectation. And the relation of *Archimedes's* lifting up the ships of *Marcellus*, among many finds but little more credit, then that of the *Gyants* shouldering *Mountains* : And yet Mathematicians know, that by multiplying of Mechanical advantages, any power may conquer any resistance, and the great *Syracusian wit* wanteth but *Tools*, and a *place* to stand on, to remove the *Earth.* So that the brag of the *Ottoman*, [*That he would throw* Malta *into the Sea*] might be performed at an easier rate, then by the shovels of his *Janizaries*.

And (2.) from this last noted head, ariseth that other of *joyning causes with irrelative effects*, which either refer not at all unto them, or in a remoter capacity. Hence the *Indian* conceiv'd so grossly of the *Letter*, that discover'd his Theft ; and that other, who thought the Watch an *Animal.* From hence grew the impostures of *Charmes*, and *Amulets*, and other insignificant ceremonies ; which to this day impose upon common belief, as they did of old upon the *Barbarism* of the incultivate *Heathen.* Thus effects unusual, whose causes run under ground, and are more remote from ordinary discernment, are noted in the Book of *Vulgar Opinion*, with *Digitus Dei*, or *Dæmonis* ; though they owe no other dependence to the *first*, then what is common to the whole *Syntax* of beings, nor yet any more to the *second*, then what is given it by the imagination of those unqualifi'd Judges. Thus

G

every unwonted *Meteor* is portentous ; and the appearance of any unobserved *Star*, some divine *Prognostick.* Antiquity thought *Thunder* the immediate voyce of *Jupiter*, and impleaded them of impiety, that referr'd it to natural causalities. Neither can there happen a *storm*, at this remove from *Antique* ignorance, but the multitude will have the *Devil* in't.

CHAP. XV.

The sixth Reason discours't of, viz. *the interest which our* Affections *have in our Dijudications. The cause why our Affections mislead us : several branches of this mention'd ; and the first,* viz. *Constitutional* Inclination *largely insisted on.*

AGAIN (6.) we owe much of our *Errour* and *Intellectual scarcity* to the Interest in, and power which our *affections* have over our so easie seducible Understandings. And 'tis a truth well worthy the Pen, from which it dropt ; *Periit Judicium, ubi res transiit in Affectum.* That *Jove* himself cannot be *wife* and in *Love* ; may be understood in a larger sense, then Antiquity meant it. *Affection* bribes the Judgement to the most notorious inequality ; and we cannot expect an equitable award, where the Judge is made a Party : So that, that understanding only is capable of giving a just decision, which is, as *Aristotle* saith of the *Law*, Νοῦς ἄνευ ὀρέξεως : But where the *Will*, or *Passion* hath the casting voyce, the case of *Truth* is *desperate*. And yet this is the miserable disorder, into which we are laps'd: The lower Powers are gotten uppermost ; and we *see* like men on our *heads*, as *Plato* observ'd of old, that on the *right* hand, which indeed is on the *left*. The *Woman* in us, still prosecutes a deceit, like that begun in the *Garden* : and our *Understandings* are wedded to an *Eve*, as fatal as the *Mother* of our *miseries*. And while all things are judged according to their suitableness, or disagreement to the *Gusto* of the fond *Feminine* ; we shall be as far from the *Tree of Knowledge*, as from that which is guarded by the *Cherubin*. The deceiver soon found this soft place of *Adam's* ; and Innocency it self did not secure him from this way of *seduction*. The first deception enter'd in at this Postern, and hath ever since kept it open for the entry of *Legion* :

G 2

so that we scarce see any thing now but through our *Passions*, the most blind, and sophisticate things about us. The *Monsters* which story relates to have their *Eyes* in their *breasts*, are *pictures* of us in our *invisible selves.* Our *Love* of one Opinion induceth us to embrace it ; and our *Hate* of another, doth more then fit us, for its rejection : And, *that Love is blind*, is extensible beyond the object of *Poetry.* When once the *affections* are engag'd, there's but a short step to the Understanding : and, *Facilè credimus quod volumus*, is a truth, that needs not plead Authority to credit it.

The reason, I conceive, is this : *Love* as it were *uniting* the Object to the *Soul*, gives it a kind of *Identity* with us ; so that the beloved *Idea* is but *our selves* in another *Name* : and when *self* is at the bar, the sentence is not like to be impartial : For every man is naturally a *Narcissus*, and each *passion* in us, no other but *self-love* sweetned by milder Epithets. We can love nothing, but what we find agreeable to our selves ; and our desire of what is *so*, hath its first inducement from within us : Yea, we love nothing but what resembleth us ;

and whatever we applaud as good or excellent, is but *self* in a *transcript*, and *è contrà*. Thus to reach the highest of our *Amours*, and to speak all at once : We love our *friends*, because they are our *Image* ; and we love our *God*, because we are *His*. So then, the *beloved* Opinion being thus wedded to the *Intellect* ; the case of our *espoused self* becomes our own : And when we weigh our selves, *Justice* doth not use to hold the ballance.

Besides, all things being double-handed, and having the appearances both of *Truth*, and *Falshood* ; where our *affections* have engaged us, we attend only to the former, which we see through a magnifying *Medium* : while looking on the latter, through the wrong end of the *Perspective*, which scants their dimensions, we neglect and contemn them. Yea, and as in corrupt judicial proceedings, the fore-stalled Understanding passes a peremptory sentence upon the single hearing of one Party ; and so though it may chance to be right in the *conclusion* ; is yet unjust and mistaken in the method of *Inference*.

But to give a more particular account of

this Imposture; our Affections engage us either,

(1.) By our Love to our Selfs : or,

(2.) By our Love to Others.

The former, in the Instances of,

(1.) *Natural disposition.*

(2.) *Custome* and *Education.*

(3.) *Interest.* And

(4.) Love of our own *Productions.*

The latter, in the homage which is paid to *Antiquity*, and *Authority.*

These are causes of our Mistakes, and Arguments that we can scarce do otherwise. And therefore I speak to them in their order.

1. *Congruity* of Opinions, whether true or false, to our *natural constitution*, is one great incentive to their reception ; For in a sense the *complexion* of the *mind*, as well as *manners*, follows the *Temperament* of the Body.   On this account some men are genially disposed to some *Opinions*, and naturally as averse to others.   And we *love* and *hate* without a known cause of either. Some Faces both of Persons and Things, we admire and dote on : others, in our impartial apprehensions no less deserving our esteem, we can not behold without resent-

ment; yea it may be with an invincible disregard. And I question not, but *intellectual* representations are received by us, with as unequal a Fate upon a bare *Temperamental* Relish or Disgust: The *Understanding* also hath its *Idiosyncrasies*, as well as other faculties. So that the great stirrs of the disputing World, are but the conflicts of the humours. *Superstition, Atheism,* and *Enthusiasm,* are tempers ; not meer infusions of *Education,* and *Opinion.* Indeed the dull and unactive spirits that concern not themselves in *Theory,* follow the swinge of the common belief in which they were first instructed : But the more *vigorous* and *stirring* will fall into *that* of their particular *Crasis.* And when the humour is awakened, all the bonds of Custome and Education cannot hold them. The opinions which are suited to their respective tempers will make way to their assent, in spight of accidental preingagements. Thus *opinions* have their *Climes* and *National* diversities : And as some Regions have their proper Vices, not so generally found in others ; so have they their mental depravities, which are drawn in with the air of their Countrey. And perhaps this is a considerable cause of the diversity of *Lawes*, *Customes*, *Religions*, *natural* and *moral* Doctrines, which is to be found in the divided Regions of the inhabited Earth. Wherefore I wonder not at the *Idolatry* of the *Jewes* of old, or of the several parts of the world to this day, at the *sensual expectation* of the *Musselmen*, the *circumstantial* follies of the *Papists*, or the antick devotions of the barbarous *Indians* ; since that the most senselesse conceits and fooleries cannot miss of Harbor, where *affection* grown upon the stock of a *depraved constitution*, hath endeared them.

And if we do but more nearly look into our *faculties*, beginning our survey from the lowest dregs of *sense*, even those which have a nearer commerce with *matter*, and so by steps ascend to our more *spiritualiz'd selves* : we shall throughly discover how *constitutional partiality* swayes us.   To begin then at the *Sences* ; that to one *Palate* is *sweet*, and *delicious*, which to another, is *odious* and *distastful* ; or more compendiously in the Proverb, *One mans meat, is anothers poyson.*   What to one is a most grateful *odour*, to another is *noxious* and *displeasant* ; and 'twere a misery to some to lye stretch't on a bed of Roses : That's a *welcome touch* to one, which is *disagreeing* to another ; The same *Aires* which some entertain with most delightful transports, to others are importune ; and the objects which *this* man can't *see* without an *Extasie, that* is no more mov'd at than a *Statue.* If we pass further, the *phancies* of men are so immediately diversify'd by the individual *Crasis,* that every man is in this a *Phœnix* ; and owns something wherein none are like him : and these are as many, as humane nature hath *singulars.* Now the *phancies* of the most, like the *Index* of a Clock, are moved but by the inward *Springs* and *Wheels* of the corporal *Machine* ; which even on the most sublimed Intellectuals is dangerously *influential.* And yet this sits at the Helm of the Worlds belief ; and Vulgar *Reason* is no better then a more *refined Imagination.* So then the *Senses, Phancy,* and what we call *Reason* it self, being thus influenc'd by the *Bodies temperament,* and little better then indications of it ; it cannot be otherwise, but that this *Love of our selves* should strongly incline us in our most *Abstracted Dijudications.*

CHAP. XVI.

A second thing whereby our Affections in-gage us in Error; is the prejudice of Custom *and* Education. *A third*, In-terest. *The fourth*, Love *to our own Pro-ductions.*

2. ANOTHER branch of this *selfish fondness*, by reason of which we miscarry of *Science*, is the almost insuper-able *prejudice* of *Custom*, and *Education*: by which our minds are encumber'd, and the most are held in a *Fatal Ignorance*. Yea could a man be composed to such an advan-tage of constitution, that it should not at all adulterate the images of his mind; yet this *second nature* would alter the *crasis* of the Understanding, and render it as obnoxi-ous to aberrances, as now. And though in the former regard, the *Soul* were a pure ἄγραφον γραμματεῖον ; yet *custom* and *edu-cation* would scrible into an incapacity of new *impressions*. Thus we judge all things by our *anticipations* ; and condemn or

applaud them, as they agree or differ from our *first receptions*. One Countrey laughs at the *Laws, Customs,* and *Opinions* of another, as absurd and ridiculous ; and the other is as charitable to them, in its conceit of theirs. This confirms the most sottish *Idolaters* in their accustomed adorations, beyond the conviction of any thing but *Dooms-day.* The impressions of a barbarous *education* are stronger in them, then *nature* ; when in their cruel *worships* they launce themselves with knifes, and expose their harmless *Infants* to the *flames* as a Sacrifice to their *Idols.* And 'tis on this account, that there's no Religion so irrational, but can boast its *Martyrs.* This is it, which befriends the *Talmud* and *Alcoran* ; and did they not owe their credit more to customary and præingag'd Assent, then to any rational inducement, we might expect their *ashes* : whereas *Education* hath so rooted these mis-believers in their ungrounded *faith*, that they may as soon be pluck't from themselves, as from their obstinate adherencies ; and to convert a *Turk*, or *Jew*, may be well a *phrase* for an attempt *impossible.* We look for it *only* from him, to whom our *Impossibles* are *none.* And 'tis to be feared

that *Christianity* it self by most, that have
espoused it, is not held by any better tenure.
The best account that many can give of
their *belief*, is, that they were *bred* in it ; and
the most are driven to their Religion by
custom and *education*, as the *Indians* are to
Baptism ; that is, like a drove of Cattle to
the water. So that had *Providence* determin'd our nativities among the Enemies of
the *Cross*, and theirs under a *Christian
horoscope* ; in all likelyhood we should have
exchang'd the Scene of our belief with that
of our abode and *breeding*. There is nothing
so absurd, to which *education* cannot form
our ductile *minority* ; it can lick us into
shapes beyond the *monstrosities* of *Africa*.
And as King *James* would say of *Parlia-
ments, It can do any thing but make a Man a
Woman*. For our initial age is like the
melted wax to the prepared Seal, capable of
any impression from the documents of our
Teachers. The *half-moon* or *Cross*, are
indifferent to its reception ; and we may
with equal facility write on this *Rasa Tabula*,
Turk, or Christian. To determine this in-
difference, our first task is to learn the *Creed*
of our Countrey ; and our next to maintain
it. We seldom examine our Receptions

more then children do their *Catechisms* ; but by a *careless greediness* swallow all at a venture. For *Implicit* faith is a vertue, where *Orthodoxie* is the object. Some will not be at the trouble of a Tryal : others are scar'd from attempting it. If we do, 'tis not by a *Sun-beam* or ray of universal light ; but by a *flame* that's kindled by our *affections*, and fed by the fewel of our *anticipations*. And thus like the *Hermite*, we think the *Sun* shines no where, but in our *Cell* ; and all the world to be darkness but ourselves. We judge truth to be circumscrib'd by the confines of our belief, and the doctrines we were brought up in : and with as ill manners, as those of *China*, repute all the rest of the world *Monoculous*. So that what some *Astrologers* say of our *Fortunes* and the passages of our lives ; may by the allowance of a *Metaphor* be said of our *Opinions* : That they are written in our *stars*, being to the most as fatal as those involuntary occurrences, and as little in their Power as the *placets* of *destiny*. We are bound to our Countreys *Opinions*, as to its *Laws* : and an accustomed assent is *tantamount* to an infallible conclusion. He that offers to dissent, shall be an *Out-law* in reputation : and the fears of guilty *Cain*, shall be fulfilled on him, who ever *meets* him *shall slay him*. Thus *Custome* and *Education* have sealed the *Canon*; and he that adds or takes away from the Book of *Orthodox* belief, shall be more then in danger of an *Anathema* : And the *Inquisition* is not confined to the jurisdiction of the *Triple-Crown*. The rankest follies are *Sacred*, if *customary*; and the *Fashion* is *handsome*, and *agreeable*, though never so *uncouth* to an unconcern'd beholder. Their *antick* deckings with *feathers* is as comly in the account of those barbarous Nations, which use them ; as the Ornaments of *Lace*, and *Ribband*, are in ours. And the plucking off the shooe is to the *Japonians* as decent a salutation, as the uncovering of the *head* is to us, and their abhorred *neighbours*. And as we are fond of every thing with which *custom* hath acquainted us ; so on the other hand we start and boggle at every *unusual* appearance, and cannot endure the sight of the *bug-bear*, *Novelty*. On this account very innocent truth's are often affix't with the reproach of *Heresie*; and made terrible things in the imaginations of their misinform'd and frighted enemies ; who like children scared in the dark, fly the *Monsters* of their *Phancies*, and dare not stay to take a true account of the object of their fears. So that there is scarce any truth, but it's adversaries have made it an ugly *Vizard*; by which it's exposed to the hate and disesteem of superficial examiners : For an opprobrious title with vulgar believers is as good as an *Argument.* And 'tis but writing the name that customary receptions have discredited, under the opinions we dislike ; and all other refutation is superfluous. Thus shallow apprehenders are frighted from many sober *Verities* ; like the King of *Arabs,* who ran away from the *smoaking Mince-Py,* apprehending some dangerous plot in the harmless steam.

So then, while we thus mistake the infusions of *education,* for the *principles* of universal *nature* ; we must needs fail of a *scientifical Theory.* And therefore the two Nations differing about the *antiquity* of their Language, made appeal to an undecisive *experiment* ; when they agreed upon the tryal of a child brought up among the wild Inhabitants of the Desert. The *Language* it spake, had no reason to be accounted the most ancient and natural : And the lucky determination for the

Phygians by its pronouncing the word *Beck*, which signified Bread in the dialect of that Countrey, they owed not to *Nature*, but the *Goat-herd* ; from which the exposed Infant, by accompanying that sort of *animals*, had learnt it.

Again (3.) *Interest* is another thing, by the *magnetisme* of which our *affections* are almost irresistibly attracted.   It is the *Pole*, to which we turn, and our *sympathizing* Judgements seldom decline from the *direction* of this *Impregnant*.   Where *Interest* hath engaged men ; they'l find a way to Truth, or make one.   Any thing is *good* and *true*, to one whose *Interest* it is, to have it so. And therefore Self-designers are seldome disappointed, for want of the speciousness of a cause to warrant them ; in the belief of which, they do oft as really impose upon themselves, as they industriously endeavour it upon others. With what an Infinite of *Law-suits, controversies,* and *litigious cases* doth the world abound? and yet every man is confident of the truth and goodness of his own.   And it may be as Master *Hobbs* observes, one   reason   that   Mathematical demonstrations are uncontroverted, is, be-

cause *Interest* hath no place in those un-
questionable *verities* : when as, did the
advantage of any stand against them,
perhaps *Euclids Elements* would not pass
with so universal a suffrage. Sir *H. Blunt*
tells us, that temporal expectations bring
in droves to the *Mahumetan Faith* ; and
we know the same holds thousands in the
Romish. The *Eagles* will be, where the
carcase is ; and that shall have the faith of
most, which is best able to pay them for't.
An advantagious cause never wanted *Prose-
lytes.* I confess, I cannot believe all the
learned *Romanists* profess against their
conscience ; but rather, that their *Interest*
brings their *consciences* to their *Profession* :
and self-advantage can as easily incline
some, to believe a falshood, as profess it.
A good *will*, help'd by a good *wit*, can
find Truth any where : and, what the
Chymists brag of their *Elixir*, it can translate any *metal* into *gold*, in the hand of a
skilful Artificer, in spight of the Adage,
Ex quolibet ligno Mercurius. Though yet
I think, that every Religion hath its bare
Nominals : and that Pope was one with
a witness, whose saying it was, *Quantum
nobis lucri peperit illa fabula de Christo* !

H

4. Besides, fourthly, *Self-love* engageth us for any thing, that is a *Minerva* of our own. And thereby detains us in the snares of *ignorance* and *folly.* We love the issues of our *Brains*, no less then those of our *bodies* : and fondness of our own *begotten notions*, though *illegitimate*, obligeth us to maintain them. We hugge intellectual deformities, if they bear our Names ; and will hardly be perswaded they are so, when our selves are their Authors. If their *Dam* may be judge, the young *Apes* are the most beautiful things in Nature ; and if we might determine it, our proper conceptions would be all voted *Axioms.* Thus then the *Female* rules, and our *Affections* wear the breeches : while our *Understandings* govern, as the story saith *Themistocles* did *Athens.* So that to give the sum of all, most of the contests of the litigious world pretending for *Truth*, are but the bandyings of one mans *affections* against anothers : in which, though their reasons may be foil'd, yet their *Passions* lose no ground, but rather improve by the *Antiperistasis* of an opposition.

CHAP. XVII.

5. *Our* Affections *are engaged by our Reverence to* Antiquity *and* Authority. *This
hath been a great hinderer of Theorical
improvements ; and it hath been an advantage to the* Mathematicks, *and* Mechanicks *Arts, that it hath no place in
them. Our mistake of* Antiquity. *The
unreasonableness of that kind of Pedantick
Adoration. Hence the vanity of affecting
impertinent quotations. The Pedantry
on't is derided ; the little improvement of
Science through its successive derivations,
and whence that hath hapned.*

ANOTHER thing, that engageth our
affections to unwarrantable conclusions, and is therefore fatal to *Science* : is
our doting on *Antiquity*, and the opinion
of our *Fathers.* We look with a supersti-
tious reverence upon the accounts of præter-
lapsed ages : and with a supercilious
severity, on the more deserving products
of our own. A vanity, which hath possess'd

H 2

all times as well as ours; and the *golden Age* was never *present.* For as in *Statick* experiment, an inconsiderable weight by virtue of its distance from the Centre of the Ballance, will preponderate much greater magnitudes; so the most slight and chaffy opinion, if at a greater remove from the present age, contracts such an esteem and veneration, that it out-weighs what is infinitely more ponderous and rational, of a *modern* date. And thus, in another sense, we realize what *Archimedes* had only in *Hypothesis*; weighing a single *grain* against the *Globe* of Earth. We reverence gray-headed Doctrines; though feeble, decrepit, and within a step of dust: and on this account maintain opinions, which have nothing but our *charity* to uphold them. While the *beauty* of a Truth, as of a *picture* is not acknowledg'd but at a *distance*; and that wisdom is nothing worth, which is not fetcht from *afar*: wherein yet we oft deceive our selves, as did that *Mariner*, who mistaking them for precious stones, brought home his ship fraught with common *Pebbles* from the remotest *Indies.* Thus our Eyes, like the *preposterous Animals*, are behind us; and our Intellectual motions

retrograde. We adhere to the determinations of our fathers, as if their *opinions*
were entail'd on us as their *lands* ; or (as
some conceive) part of the Parents soul
were portion'd out to his off-spring, and the
conceptions of our minds were *ex traduce.*
The Sages of old live again in us ; and in
opinions there is a *Metempsychosis.* We
are our re-animated *Ancestours,* and antedate their *Resurrection.*

And thus, while every age is but another
shew of the former ; 'tis no wonder, that Science hath not out-grown the dwarfishness of
its *pristine stature,* and that the *Intellectual
world* is such a *Microcosm.* For while we
account of some admired Authors, as the
Seths Pillars, on which all knowledge is
engraven ; and spend that time and study in
defence of their Placets, which with more
advantage to Science might have been employ'd upon the Books of the more ancient,
and *universal Author* : 'Tis not to be
admired, that Knowledge hath receiv'd so
little improvement from the endeavours of
many pretending promoters, through the
continued series of so many successive ages.
For while we are slaves to the *Dictates* of
our *Progenitours* ; our discoveries, like

water, will not run higher then the *Fountains*, from which they own their derivation. And while we think it so piaculous, to go beyond the *Ancients* ; we must necessarily come short of genuine *Antiquity*, *Truth* ; unless we suppose them to have reach'd perfection of knowledge in spight of their own acknowledgements of *Ignorance*.

Now if we enquire the reason, why the *Mathematicks*, and *Mechanick Arts*, have so much got the start in growth of other *Sciences* : we shall find it probably resolv'd into this, as one considerable cause : that their progress hath not been retarded by that reverential awe of former discoveries, which hath been so great an hinderance to Theorical improvements. 'Twas never an heresie to out-limn *Apelles* ; nor criminal to out-work the *Obelisks*. *Galilæus* without a crime out-saw all *Antiquity*, and was not afraid to believe his eyes, in spight of the *Opticks* of *Ptolomy* and *Aristotle*. 'Tis no discredit to the *Telescope* that Antiquity ne're saw in't : Nor are we shy of assent to those *celestial* informations, because they were *hid from ages*. We believe the *verticity* of the *Needle*, without a Certificate from the *dayes of old* : And confine not our selves to the sole conduct of the *Stars*, for fear of being wiser then our Fathers. Had *Authority* prevail'd here, the Earths *fourth part* had to us been none, and *Hercules* his Pillars had still been the worlds *Non ultra* : *Seneca's* Prophesie had been an unfulfill'd Prediction, and one moiety of our *Globes*, an empty *Hemisphere.*

In a sense, **Tὰ** ἀρχαῖα κρατείτω, is a wholesom instruction ; and becoming the Vote of a *Synod* : But yet, in common acceptation, it's an Enemy to Verity, which can plead the *antiquity* of above *six thousand* ; and bears date from before the *Chaos.* For, as the Noble Lord *Verulam* hath noted, we have a mistaken apprehension of *Antiquity* ; calling that so, which in truth is the worlds Nonage. *Antiquitas seculi est juventus Mundi.* So that in such appeals, we fetch our knowledge from the *Cradle* ; which though it be nearest to *Innocence*, it is so too to the fatal ruines which follow'd it. Upon a true account, the *present age* is the worlds *Grandævity* ; and if we must to *Antiquity, Let multitude of dayes speak.* Now for us to supersede further disquisition, upon the immature acquirements of those Juvenile endeavours, is foolishly to neglect the nobler advantages we are owners of, and in a sense to disappoint the expectations of him that gave them. Yet thus hath the world prevented it self of *Science.* And *aged* Knowledge, is still an *Infant.* We *superstitiously* sit down in the Acquisitions of our Fathers ; and are discouraged from attempting further then they have gone before us. So that, but for the undertakings of some glorious persons, who now and then shine upon the world, *Plato's* year might have found us, where the dayes of *Aristotle* left us. For my part, I think it no such arrogance, as some are pleased to account it, that almost two thousand years elapsed since, should *weigh* with the *sixty three* of the *Stagirite.* If we owe it to him, that we know so much ; 'tis perhaps long of his fond adorers that we know so little more. I can see no ground, why his Reason should be *textuary* to ours ; or that God, or Nature, ever intended him an Universal *Headship.* 'Twas this vain Idolizing of Authors, which gave birth to that silly vanity of *impertinent citations* ; and inducing *Authority* in things neither requiring, nor deserving it. That saying was much more observable, *That men have beards, and women none* ; because

quoted from *Beza* : and that other, *Pax res
bona est* ; because brought in with a, *said*
St. *Augustine.* But these ridiculous fooleries, signifie nothing to the more generous
discerners, but the *Pedantry* of the affected
Sciolist. 'Tis an inglorious acquist to have
our heads or Volumes laden, as were Car-
dinal *Campeius* his Mules, with old and
useless luggage : And yet the magnificence
of many high pretenders to Science, if laid
open by a true discovery, would amount to
no more then the old *Boots* and *Shooes*, of
that proud, and exposed *Embassadour.*
Methinks 'tis a pitiful piece of Knowledge,
that can be learnt from an *Index* ; and a
poor Ambition to be rich in the Inventory of
anothers Treasure. To boast a *memory* (the
most that these Pedants can aim at) is but
an humble ostentation. And of all the
faculties, in which some Brutes out-vie us, I
least envy them an excellence in that ;
desiring rather to be a *Fountain* then an
Hogs-head. 'Tis better to own a Judgment,
though but with a *Curta supellex* of coherent
notions ; then a *memory*, like a Sepulchre,
furnished with a load of broken and dis-
carnate bones. *Authorities* alone with me
make no *number*, unless Evidence of Reason

stand before them : For all the *Cyphers* of *Arithmatick*, are no better then a single *nothing.* And yet this rank folly of affecting such impertinencies, hath overgrown our Times ; and those that are Candidates for the repute of *Scholars*, take this way to compass it. When as multiplicity of reading, the best it can signifie, doth but speak them to have taken pains for it : And this alone is but the dry and barren part of Knowledge, and hath little reason to denominate. A number of *Receipts* at the best can but make an *Emperick.* But again, to what is more perpendicular to our discourse, if we impartially look into the remains of *Antique* Ages ; we shall find but little to justifie so groundless a Tyranny, as *Antiquity* hath impos'd on the enslaved world. For if we take an account of the state of *Science*, beginning as high as History can carry us ; we shall find it still to have lain under such unhappy disadvantages, as have hindred it's advance in any considerable degrees of improvement. And though it hath oft chang'd its Channel, by its remove from one Nation to another ; yet hath it been little more alter'd, then a *River* in its passage through differing *Regions, viz.* in

Name and *Method.* For the succeeding
times still subscribing to, and copying out
those, who went before them, with little more
then *verbal* diversity ; *Science* hath still been
the same *pitiful* thing, though in a various
Livery. The *Græcian* learning was but a
transcript of the *Chaldæan* and *Ægyptian* ;
and the *Roman* of the *Græcian.* And
though those former dayes have not wanted
brave *Wits*, that have gallantly attempted,
and made Essays worthy Immortality ; yet
by reason either of the unqualified capacities
of the multitude, (who dote on things slight
and trivial, neglecting what is more rare and
excellent) or the clamorous assaults of
envious and more popular opposers, they
have submitted to Fate, and are almost lost
in *Oblivion.* And therefore, as that great
man, the *Lord Bacon* hath observ'd, *Time* as
a *River*, hath brought down to us what is
more light and superficial ; while things
more solid and substantial have been im-
mersed. Thus the *Aristotelian Philosophy*
hath prevailed ; while the more excellent
and more *Antient Atomical Hypothesis* hath
long lain buryed in neglect and darkness ;
and for ought I know, might have slept for
ever, had not the ingenuity of the present

age, recal'd it from its *urne* and *silence* But
it is somewhat collateral to my scope, as
well as disproportion'd to my abilities, to fall
upon particular Instances of the defects and
Errours of the *Philosophy* of the *Antients.*
The foremention'd noble *Advancer of Learning*, whose name and parts might give
credit to any undertaking ; hath handsomely
perform'd it, in his ingenious *Novum
Organum.* And yet, because it may confer
towards the discovery of how little our adherence to *Antiquity* befriends *Truth*, and
the encrease of Knowledge ; as also how
groundless are the *Dogmatists* high pretensions to *Science* : I shall adventure some considerations on the *Peripatetick Philosophy* ;
which hath had the luck to survive all others,
and to build a fame on their *Ruines.*

CHAP. XVIII.

REFLEXIONS on the PERIPATETICK PHILOSOPHY.

The Generality of its Reception, no Argument of its deserts ; the first charge against that Philosophy ; that it is meerly verbal. Materia prima *in that Philosophy signifies nothing. A Parallel drawn between it and Imaginary Space : this latter pleads more for its reality. Their* Form *also is a meer word, and* potentia Materiæ *insignificant.* Privation *no* principle. *An essay to detect Peripatetick Verbosity, by translating some definitions.*

HOW *Aristotles Philosophy* came so universally to obtain in these later Ages, to the silencing the *Zoroastrian, Pythagorean, Platonical,* and *Epicurean* Learning, is not my business here to inquire. Worth is not to be judg'd by Success, and Retinue ; only we may take notice, that the *Generality* of it's *reception* is with many the *perswading* Argument of it's *superlative* desert.   And common Judges measure *excellency* by *Name* and *Numbers*. But *Seneca's* determination, *Argumentum pessimi Turba est*, is more deserving our credit : and the *fewest*, that is the *wisest*, have alwayes stood contradictory to that ground of belief ; Vulgar applause by severer Wisdom being held a scandal.   If the numerousness of a Train must carry it ; *Virtue* may go follow *Astræa*, and *Vice* only will be worth the courting.   The *Philosopher* deservedly suspected himself of vanity, when cryed up by the multitude : And discreet apprehenders will not think the better of that *Philosophy*, which hath the common cry to vouch it.   He that writ counter to the *Astrologer* in his *Almanack*, did with more truth foretell the *weather* : and he that shall write *Foul*, in the place of the Vulgars *Fair* ; passes the juster censure.   Those in the *Fable*, who were wet with the showre of *folly*, hooted at the *wise men* that escap'd it, and pointed at their actions as *ridiculous* ; because unlike their own, that were truly *so*.   If the major Vote may cast it, *Wisdom* and *Folly* must exchange names ; and the way to the one will be by the other.   Nor is it the Rabble

only, which are such perverse discerners ;
we are now a sphear above them : I mean
the τὸ πολὺ of pretended *Philosophers*, who
judge as odly in their way, as the *Rascality*
in theirs ; and many a profest Retainer to
Philosophy, is but an *Ignoramus* in a suit
of *second Notions.* 'Tis such, that most
revere the Reliques of the Adored *Sophy* ;
and, as *Artemesia* did those of *Mausolus*,
passionately drink his *ashes.* Whether the
Remains of the *Stagirite* deserve such
Veneration, we'll make a brief enquiry.

In the conduct of which design, 6 Things
I offer against that *Philosophy, viz.* (1.)
That 'tis meerly *Verbal*, and (2.) *Litigious.*
That (3.) It gives no account of the *Phænomena.* Nor (4.) doth it make any *discoveries* for the *use* of common *Life.* That
(5.) 'tis inconsistent with *Divinity*, and (6.)
with it *self.* Which charges how just they
are, I think will appear in the sequell.

To the *First* then. That the *Aristotelian
Philosophy* is an huddle of *words* and *terms
insignificant*, hath been the censure of the
wisest : And that both its *Basis* and *Superstructure* are *Chimærical* ; cannot be un-
observ'd by them, that know it, and are
free to judge it. To detect the verbal

Emptiness of this *Philosophy*, I'le begin at the Foundation of the *Hypothesis*. For I intend but *few*, and those shall be *signal Instances*.

(1.) Therefore the *Materia prima* of this *Philosophy*, shall be that of my *Reflections*. In the consideration of which I shall need no more then the notion wherein *Aristotle* himself hath drest it ; for evidence of what I aim at ; for, *Nec quid, nec quale, nec quantum*, is as opposite a definition of *Nothing*, as can be. So that if we would conceive this *Imaginary Matter*, we must deny all things of it, that we can conceive ; and what remains is the thing we look for. And allowing all which its Assertors assign it, *viz. Quantity interminate* ; 'tis still but an empty extended capacity, and therefore at the best, but like that *Space*, which we imagine was before the beginning of *Time*, and will be after *It*. 'Tis easie to draw a *Parallelism* between that *Ancient*, and this more *Modern Nothing* ; and in all things to make good its resemblance to that *Commentitious Inanity*. The *Peripatetick matter* is a pure unactuated Power : and this conceited *Vacuum* a meer Receptibility. *Matter* is suppos'd *indeterminate* : and *Space* is *so*. The pretended *first matter* is capable of all *forms* : And the *imaginary space* is receptive of any *body*. *Matter* cannot naturally subsist *uninform'd* : And *Nature* avoids *vacuity* in *space*. The *matter* is *ingenerate*, and beyond corruption : And the *space* was before, and will be after either. The *matter* in all things is but *one* : and the *space* most *uniform*. Thus the Foundation-Principle of *Peripateticism* is exactly parallel to an acknowledg'd *nothing* : and their agreement in essential characters makes rather an *Identity* then a *Parity* ; but that *Imaginary space* hath more to plead for its *reality*, then the *matter* hath, and in this consists the greatest dissimilitude. For *that* hath no dependence on the bodies which possess it ; but was before them, and will survive them : whereas *this* essentially relies on the *form* and cannot subsist without it. Which yet, me thinks, is little better than an *absurdity* : that the cause should be an *Eleemosynary* for its subsistence to its effect, and a nature *posterior* to, and dependent on it self. This *dependentia a posteriori*, though in a diverse way of causality, my reason could never away with : yea, a Sectator of this *Philo-*

I

sophy, Oviedo a *Spanish* Jesuite, hath effectually impugn'd it.   So then there's nothing *real*, answering this Imaginary *Proteus*; and *Materia prima* hath as much of being, as *Mons aureus.*

(2.) The *Peripatetick Forms* are as obnoxious, and on the same account lyable to our Reflections as the former Principle.   I'le not spend time in an industrious confutation of what the Votaries of that *Philosophy* themselves can scarce tell what to make of : And the subject being dry and less sutable to those more *Mercurial* tempers for whom I intend these Papers : I'le only pass a Reflection on it, and proceed to what may be less importunate.

The *Form* then, according to this *Hypothesis*, is a new substance produced in all generations to actuate the *Matter* and *Passive* Principle ; out of whose *Power* 'tis said to be educed.   And were it supposed to contain any thing of the *Form* præexisting in it, as the seed of the *Being* to be produced ; 'twere then sense to say, It was *Educed* from it ; but by *Educing*, the affirmers only mean a producing in it, with a subjective dependence on its Recipient : a *worthy* signification of *Eduction*; which answers not the question whence 'tis derived, but into what it is received. The question is of the *terminus à quo*, and the answer of the *subject*. So that all that can be made of this *power* of the *matter*, is meerly *a receptive capacity*: and we may as well affirm that the world was *educ'd* out of the *power* of the *imaginary space*; and give that as a sufficient account of its Original. And in this language, to grow rich were to *educe* money out of the *power* of the Pocket. Wherefore, notwithstanding this *Imaginary Eduction* out of the *power* of the *Matter*; we are still to seek whether these *Forms* be produced out of *something*, or *nothing*; either of which supposed, bids defiance to the *Hypothesis*. For according to the first, all possible Forms will be actually latent in the Matter; which is contrary to the stream of the *Peripatetick* Doctors. And the latter as opposite to their Master's *Ex Nihilo Nihil*, and he acknowledged no *Creation*.

(3.) The third *Principle* of *Bodies* according to the *Aristotelian Philosophy* is *Privation*; concerning which, I'le add nothing but the words of the excellent Lord *Montaigne*,

Qu'est il plus vain que de faire l' inanité mesme, cause de la production des choses ? La privation c'est une negative: de quel humeur en a-il peu faire la cause & origine des choses qui sont ?

But yet further, to give an hint more of the *Verbosities* of this *Philosophy*, a short view of a definition or two will be sufficient evidence; which, though in *Greek* or *Latin* they amuse us ; yet a Translation unmasks them. And if we make them speak *English*, the cheat is transparent.

Light is **ΕΝΕΡΓΙΑ ΤΟΥ ΔΙΑΦΑΝΟΥ** saith that *Philosophy* : In English, the *Act of a perspicuous Body.* Sure *Aristotle* here transgres't his own *Topicks*, and if this *Definition* be clearer and more known then the thing *defined*, *Midnight* may vie for *conspicuity* with *Noon.* Is not Light more known then this insignificant *Energy?* And what's a *diaphanous* body, but the Lights *medium* the *Air?* so that *Light* is the *Act of the Air.* And if *Lux* be *Umbra Dei*, this definition is *Umbra Lucis.* Thus is Light darkened by an illustration, and the *symbol* of *evidence*, cloathed in the Livery of *Midnight* : As if *light* were best seen by *darkness*, as *Light inaccessible* is best *known* by *Ignorance.*

Again (2.) That *Motion* is ENTEΛEXEIA TOY ONTOΣ EN ΔYNAMEI, *&c.* is a definition of *Aristotle's*, and as culpable as the former. For, by the most favourable interpretation of that unintelligible *Entelechy* : It is but, *An act of a-being in power, as it is in power* ; the construing of which into palpable sense or meaning would poze a Critick. Sure that *Definition* is not very *conspicuous*, whose *Genus* puzzled the *Devil.* The *Philosopher* that prov'd *motion* by walking, did in that action better *define* it : And that puzled *Candidate*, who being ask'd what a *circle* was, describ'd it by the *rotation* of his *hand* ; gave an account more satisfying. In some things we must indeed give an allowance for words of Art : But in defining obvious appearances, we are to use what is most plain and easie ; that the mind be not misled by *Amphibologies*, or ill conceived notions, into fallacious deductions : which whether it be not the method of *Peripatetick Philosophy* let the indifferent determine. To give an account of all the insignificancies, and verbal nothings of this *Philosophy*, would be almost to transcribe it. 'Tis a *Philosophy*, that makes most accurate Inspections into the *Creatures* of the *Brain*; and gives the exactest *Topography* of the *Extramundane spaces*. Like our late *Polititians*, it makes discoveries, and their objects too ; and deals in beings, that owe nothing to the *Primitive Fiat.* The same undivided Essence, from the several circumstances of its being and operations, is here multiplyed into *Legion*, and emprov'd to a number of smaller *Entities* ; and these again into as many *Modes* and insignificant *formalities*. What a number of words here have nothing answering them ? and as many are imposed at random. To wrest names from their known meaning to Senses most alien, and to darken *speech by words without knowledge* ; are none of the most inconsiderable faults of this *Philosophy* : To reckon them in their particular instances, would puzzle *Archimedes*. Now hence the genuine *Idea's* of the mind are adulterate : and the Things themselves lost in a crowd of *Names*, and *Intentional nothings*. Besides, these *Verbosities* emasculate the understanding ; and render it slight and frivolous, as its objects.

Methinks, the late *Voluminous Jesuits*, those *Laplanders* of *Peripateticism*, do but subtilly trifle, and their *Philosophick* understandings are much like his, who spent his time in darting *Cumming-seed* through the *Eye* of a *Needle.* One would think they were impregnated, as are the Mares in *Cappadocia* ; they are big of words : their tedious Volumes have the *Tympany,* and bring forth nought but wind, and vapour. To me, a *cursus Philosophicus,* is but an Impertinency in *Folio* ; and the studying them a *laborious idleness.* 'Tis here, that things are crumbled into *notional Atomes* ; and the substance evaporated into an *imaginary Æther.* The intellect that can feed on this *air,* is a *Chamæleon* ; and a meer *inflated* skin. From this stock grew *School-Divinity,* which is but *Peripateticism* in a *Theological Livery.* A *School-man* is the Ghost of the *Stagirite,* in a Body of condensed Air : and *Thomas* but *Aristotle Sainted.*

2. Peripatetick Philosophy *is* Litigious; *it hath no setled constant signification of words; the inconveniences hereof.* Aristotle *intended the cherishing controversies; prov'd by his own double testimony. Some of his impertinent arguings instanc't in. Disputes retard, and are injurious to knowledge. Peripateticks are most exercised in the* Controversal *parts of Philosophy, and know little of the* practical *and* experimental. *A touch at School-Divinity.*

BUT (2.) this *Philosophy* is *litigious*, the very spawn of *disputations* and *controversies* as undecisive as needless. This is the natural result of the former : *Storms* are the products of *vapours*. For where *words* are imposed *arbitrariously*, having no stated real meaning ; or else distorted from their common use, and known significations ; the mind must needs be led into confusion and misprision ; and so things plain and easie in their naked natures, made full of *intricacy* and disputable *uncertainty.* For we cannot conclude with assurance, but from clearly apprehended *premises* ; and these cannot be so conceiv'd, but by a *distinct* comprehension of the *words* out of which they are *elemented.* So that, where these are unfixt or ambiguous ; our *propositions* must be so, and our *deductions* can be no better. One reason therefore of the uncontroverted certainty of *Mathematical Science* is ; because 'tis built upon clear and settled *significations* of *names*, which admit of no *ambiguity* or insignificant *obscurity.* But in the *Aristotelian* Philosophy it's quite otherwise : Words being here carelesly and abusively admitted, and as inconstantly retained ; it must needs come to pass, that they will be diversly apprehended by contenders, and so made the subject of *Controversies*, that are *endless* both for *use* and *number.* And thus being at their first step out of the way to *Science*, by mistaking in *simple terms* ; in the progress of their enquiries they must needs lose both themselves, and the Truth, in a *Verbal Labyrinth.* And now the entangled Disputants, as Master *Hobs* ingeniously observeth, like Birds that came down the Chimney ; betake them to the false light, seldom suspecting the way they entr'd : But attempting by vain, impertinent, and coincident distinctions, to escape the absurdity that pursues them ; do but weary themselves with as little success, as the silly Bird attempts the window. The mis-stated words are the original mistake ; and every other essay is a new one.

Now these canting contests, the usual entertainment of the *Peripatum*, are not only the accidental *vitiosities* of the *Philosophers* ; but the genuine issues of the *Philosophy* it self. And *Aristotle* seems purposely to intend the cherishing of *controversal digladiations*, by his own affectation of an intricate *obscurity*. Himself acknowledg'd, when he said ; his *Physicks* were *publish'd*, and not *so* : And by that double advice in his *Topicks* 'tis as clear as light. In one place, he adviseth his Sectatours in disputations to be *ambiguous* : and in another, to bring forth anything that occurs, rather than give way to their Adversary : Counsel very well becoming an Enquirer into Truth and Nature. Nor did he here advise them to any thing, but what he followeth himself, and exactly copies out in his practice : The multitudes of the *lame, abrupt, equivocal*,

self-contradicting expressions, will evidence
it as to the first part : which who considers,
may be satisfied in this ; that if *Aristotle*
found *Natures face* under covert of a *veil,* he
hath not removed the old, but made her a
new one. And for the latter, his frequent
slightness in arguing doth abundantly make
it good. To instance :

He proves the *world* to be perfect, because
it consists of *bodies* ; and that *bodies* are so,
because they consist of a *triple dimension* ;
and that a *triple dimension* is perfect, because *three* are *all* ; and that *three* are *all,*
because when 'tis but *one* or *two,* we can't
say *all,* but when 'tis *three,* we may : Is not
this an absolute *demonstration?* We can
say All at the number *three* : Therefore the
world is perfect. Tobit went forth and his
Dog follow'd him ; therefore there's a *world*
in the *Moon,* were an argument as *Apodic-
tical.* In another place (2.) he proves the
world to be but *one* : For were there
another, our Earth would fall unto it. Which
is but a pitiful deduction, from the meer
prejudice of *Sense* ; and not unlike theirs,
who thought, if there were *Antipodes,* they
must needs (as it's said of *Erasmus*) *in
Cælum descendere.* As if, were there more

worlds, each of them would not have its proper *Centre*.   Else-where (3.) shewing, why the *Heavens* move this way rather than another, he gives this for a reason :   because they move to the more *honourable* ; and *before* is more *honourable* then *after*.   This is like the *Gallant*, who sent his man to buy an *Hat*, that would *turn up behind*.   As if, had the Heavens moved the other way ; that term had not been then *before*, which is now the contrary.   This inference is founded upon a very weak supposition, *viz.*   That those alterable respects are realities in Nature ; which will never be admitted by a considerate discerner.   Thus *Aristotle* acted his own instructions ; and his obsequious Sectators have super-erogated in observance.   They have so disguised his *Philosophy* by obscuring *Comments*, that his revived self would not own it :   And were he to act another part with mortals, he'd be but a pitiful *Peripatetick* ; every *Sophister* would out-talk him.

Now the *disputing* way of Enquiry is so far from advancing *Science* ; that 'tis no inconsiderable retarder :   For in *Scientifical* discoveries many things must be consider'd, which the hurry of a dispute indisposeth for;

and there is no way to *Truth*, but by the
most clear comprehension of *simple notions*,
and as wary an accuracy in *deductions*. If
the Fountain be disturb'd, there's no seeing
to the bottom ; and here's an exception to
the Proverb, *'Tis no good fishing for* Verity
in troubled waters. One mistake of either
simple apprehension, or *connexion*, makes an
erroneous conclusion. So that the precipitancy of *disputation*, and the stir and noise of
Passions, that usually attend it, must needs
be prejudicial to Verity : its calm insinu-
ations can no more be heard in such a bustle,
then a whisper among a croud of Saylors in
a storm. Nor do the eager clamors of contending Disputants, yield any more relief to
eclipsed Truth ; then did the sounding Brass
of old to the *labouring Moon.* When it's
under question, 'twere as good slip *cross* and
pile, as to dispute for't : and to play a game
at *Chess* for an opinion in *Philosophy* (as my
self and an ingenious Friend have sometimes sported) is as likely a way to determine.
Thus the *Peripatetick* procedure is inept for
Philosophical solutions :   The *Lot* were as
equitable a decision, as their empty *Loqua-
cities.*

'Tis these ungracious *Disputations* that

have been the great hinderance to the more improvable parts of Learning : and the modern Retainers to the *Stagirite* have spent their sweat and pains upon the most litigious parts of his *Philosophy* ; while those, that find less play for the contending *Genius*, are incultivate. Thus *Logick*, *Physicks*, and *Metaphysicks*, are the burden of Volumes, and the dayly entertainment of the *Disputing Schools* : while the more profitable doctrines of the *Heavens*, *Meteors*, *Minerals*, *Animals* ; as also the more *practical* ones of *Politicks*, and *Oeconomicks*, are scarce so much as glanc'd at. And the indisputable *Mathematicks*, the only *Science* Heaven hath yet vouchsaf't Humanity, have but few Votaries among the slaves of the *Stagirite*. What, the late promoters of the *Aristotelian Philosophy*, have writ on all these so fertile subjects, can scarce compare with the single disputes about *Materia prima*.

Nor hath Humane Science monopoliz'd the damage, that hath sprung from this Root of Evils : *Theology* hath been as deep a sharer. The Volumes of the *Schoolmen*, are deplorable evidence of *Peripatetick depravations* : And *Luther's* censure of that

Divinity, Quam primum apparuit Theologia Scholastica, evanuit Theologia Crucis, is neither uncharitable, nor unjust. This hath mudded the Fountain of Certainty with notional and Ethnick admixtions, and platted the head of *Evangelical* truth, as the *Jews* did its *Author's,* with a *Crown* of *Thorns* : Here, the most obvious Verity is subtiliz'd into niceties, and spun into a thread indiscernible by common *Opticks,* but through the *spectacles* of the Adored *Heathen.* This hath robb'd the *Christian* world of its *unity* and *peace,* and made the Church, the Stage of everlasting contentions : And while *Aristotle* is made the *Center* of *Truth,* and *Unity,* what hope of reconciling? And yet most of these Scholastick controversies are ultimately resolv'd into the subtilties of his *Philosophy* : whereas me thinks an *Athenian* should not be the best guide to the ΘΕΟΣ ΑΓΝΩΣΤΟΣ ; Nor an *Idolater* to that God he neither knew nor owned. When I read the eager contests of those *Notional Theologues,* about things that are not ; I cannot but think of that pair of *wise ones,* that fought for the *middle* : And me thinks many of their Controversies are such, as if *we* and our *Antipodes,* should strive who were *uppermost* ; their Title to Truth is equal. He that divided his *Text* into *one part* ; did but imitate the *Schoolmen* in their *coincident distinctions* : And the best of their *curiosities* are but like paint on Glass, which intercepts and dyes the light the more desirable splendor. I cannot look upon their elaborate trifles, but with a sad reflexion on the degenerate state of our lapsed Intellects ; and as deep a resentment, of the mischiefs of this *School-Philosophy.*

3. *It gives no account of the* Phænomena ; *those that are remoter, it attempts not. It speaks nothing pertinent in the most ordinary : Its circular, and general way of Solution. It resolves all things into* occult *qualities. The absurdity of the* Aristotelian *Hypothesis of the Heavens. The* Galaxy *is no* Meteor : *the* Heavens *are* corruptible. Comets *are above the* Moon. *The* Sphear *of* fire *derided.* Aristotle *convicted of several other false assertions.*

3. THE *Aristotelian Hypotheses* give a very dry and *jejune* account of Nature's *Phænomena.*

For (1.) as to its more *mysterious* reserves, *Peripatetick* enquiry hath left them unattempted ; and the most forward notional Dictators sit down here in a contented ignorance : and as if nothing more were knowable then is already discover'd, they

K

put stop to all endeavours of their Solution. *Qualities*, that were *Occult* to *Aristotle*, must be *so* to us ; and we must not *Philosophize* beyond *Sympathy* and *Antipathy* : whereas indeed the *Rarities* of Nature are in these *Recesses*, and its most excellent operations *Cryptick* to common discernment. Modern Ingenuity expects Wonders from *Magnetick* discoveries : And while we know but its more sensible wayes of working ; we are but vulgar *Philosophers*, and not likely to help the *World* to any considerable *Theories*. Till the *Fountains* of the great *deeps* are broken up ; *Knowledge* is not likely to cover the *Earth* as the waters the *Sea*.

Nor (2.) is the *Aristotelian Philosophy* guilty of this sloth and Philosophick penury, only in remoter abstrusities : but in solving the most *ordinary causalities*, it is as defective and unsatisfying. Even the most common productions are here resolv'd into *Celestial influences*, *Elemental combinations*, *active* and *passive* principles, and such *generalities* ; while the particular manner of them is as hidden as *sympathies*. And if we follow *manifest qualities* beyond the empty signification of their Names; we shall find them as *occult*, as those which are professedly *so*. That heavy Bodies descend by *gravity*, is no better an account then we might expect from a *Rustick*: and again, that *Gravity* is a *quality* whereby an heavy body descends, is an impertinet *Circle*, and teacheth nothing. The feigned *Central alliciency* is but a word, and the manner of it still *occult*. That the *fire* burns by a quality called *heat*; is an empty dry return to the Question, and leaves us still ignorant of the immediate way of *Igneous solutions*. The accounts that this *Philosophy* gives by other *Qualities*, are of the same *Gender* with these: So that to say the *Loadstone* draws *Iron* by *magnetick attraction*, and that the *Sea* moves by *flux* and *reflux*; were as satisfying as these *Hypotheses*, and the solution were as pertinent. In the *Qualities*, this Philosophy calls *manifest*, nothing is *so* but the effects. For the *heat*, we feel, is but the *effect* of the *fire*; and the *pressure*, we are sensible of, but the *effect* of the *descending* body. And effects, whose causes are confessedly *occult*, are as much within the sphear of our Senses; and our Eyes will inform us of the motion of the Steel to its

K 2

attrahent. Thus *Peripatetick Philosophy*
resolves all things into *Occult qualities*;
and the *Dogmatists* are the only *Scepticks.*
Even to them, that pretend so much to
Science, the world is circumscrib'd with a
Gyges his ring; and is *intellectually invisible* : And, ΟΥ ΚΑΤΑΛΑΜΒΑΝΩ, is a fit
Motto for the *Peripatum.* For by their way
of disquisition there can no more be truly
comprehended, then what's known by every
common Ignorant. And ingenious inquiry
will not be contented with such vulgar
frigidities.

But further, (3.) if we look into the
Aristotelian Comments on the largest
Volumes of the Universe : The works of
the *fourth day* are there as confused and
disorderly, as the *Chaos* of the *first* : and
more like that, which was before the *light*,
then the compleatly finish'd, and gloriously
disposed *frame.* What a *Romance* is the
story of those impossible *concamerations,
Intersections, Involutions,* and feign'd *Rotations* of *solid Orbs?* All substituted to
salve the credit of a broken ill-contrived
Systeme. The belief of such disorders
above, were an advantage to the *oblique*

Atheism of *Epicurus* : And such Irregularities in the Celestial motions, would lend an
Argument to the *Apotheiosis* of *Fortune.*
Had the world been coagmented from that
supposed fortuitous Jumble ; this *Hypothesis*
had been tolerable. But to intitle such
abrupt, confused motions to *Almighty
wisdom,* is to degrade it below the size of
humane forecast and contrivance. And
could the doctrine of *solid Orbs,* be accommodated to *Astronomical Phænomena* ; yet
to ascribe each *Sphear* an *Intelligence* to
circumvolve it, were an *unphilosophical*
desperate refuge : And to confine the blessed
Genii to a Province, which was the *Hell* of
Ixion, were to rob them of their *Felicities.*
That the *Galaxy* is a *Meteor,* was the account of *Aristotle* : But the *Telescope* hath
autoptically confuted it : And he, who is not
Pyrrhonian to the dis-belief of his Senses,
may see, that it's no exhalation from the
Earth, but an heap of smaller *Luminaries.*
That the *Heavens* are void of *corruption,* is
Aristotles supposal : But the Tube hath
betray'd their impurity ; and *Neoterick
Astronomy* hath found *spots* in the *Sun.*
The discoveries made in *Venus,* and the
Moon, disprove the *Antique Quintessence* ;

and evidence them of as course *materials*,
as the *Globe* we belong to. The *Perspicil*,
as well as the *Needle*, hath enlarged the
habitable World; and that the *Moon* is an
Earth, is no improbable conjecture. The
inequality of its surface, *Mountanous pro-
tuberance*, the nature of its *Maculæ*, and
infinite other circumstances (for which the
world's beholding to *Galilæo*) are Items not
contemptible : *Hevelius* hath *graphically*
described it : That *Comets* are of nature
Terrestrial, is allowable : But that they are
material'd of vapours, and never flamed
beyond the *Moon* ; were a concession un-
pardonable. That in *Cassiopæa* was in the
Firmanent, and another in our age above
the *Sun.* Nor was there ever any as low as
the highest point of the *circumference*, the
Stagyrite allows them. So that we need not
be appall'd at *Blazing Stars*, and a *Comet* is
no more ground for *Astrological presages*
then a *flaming* Chimney. The unparallel d
Des-Cartes hath unridled their dark *Physiology*, and to wonder solv'd their *Motions.*
His *Philosophy* gives them transcursions
beyond the *Vortex* we breath in ; and leads
them through others, which are only known
in an *Hypothesis. Aristotle* would have

fainted before he had flown half so far, as that *Eagle-wit* ; and have lighted on a *hard name*, or *occult quality*, to rest him. That there is a *sphear* of *fire* under the concave of the *Moon*, is a dream : And this, may be, was the reason some imagin'd *Hell* there, thinking those flames the *Ignis Rotæ*. According to this *Hypothesis*, the whole *Lunar* world is a *Torrid Zone* ; and on a better account, then *Aristotle* thought ours was, may be supposed *inhabitable*, except they are *Salamanders* which dwell in those *fiery Regions*. That the *Reflexion* of the *Solar* Rays, is terminated in the *Clouds* ; was the opinion of the *Grœcian Sage* : But *Lunar* observations have convicted it of falshood ; and that Planet receives the *dusky* light, we discern in its *Sextile Aspect*, from the *Earth's* benignity. That the *Rainbow* never describes more then a *semicircle*, is no credible assertion ; since experimental observations have confuted it. *Gassendus* saw one at Sun-setting, whose Supreme *Arch* almost reached our *Zenith*, while the Horns stood in the *Oriental Tropicks*. And that Noble wit reprehends the *School-Idol*, for assigning fifty years at least between every *Lunar Iris*. That *Caucasus* enjoys the

Sunbeams three parts of the Nights *Vigils* ; that *Danubius* ariseth from the *Pyrenæan* Hills : That the Earth is higher towards the *North* : are opinions truly charged on *Aristotle* by the *Restorer* of *Epicurus* ; and all easily confutable falsities. To reckon all the *Aristotelian* aberrances, and to give a full account of the lameness of his *Hypotheses*, would swell this *digression* into a Volume. The mention'd shall suffice us.

4. Aristotle's *Philosophy inept for new discoveries; it hath been the Author of no
one invention : It's founded on vulgarities,
and therefore makes nothing known beyond them.* The *knowledge of Natures
outside confers not to practical improvements.* Better *hopes from the New
Philosophy.* The *directing all this to
the design of the Discourse.* A *Caution,*
viz. *that nothing is here intended in
favour of* novelty *in* Divinity ; *the reason
why we may embrace what is new in*
Philosophy, *while we reject them in
Theologie.*

4. THE *Aristotelian Philosophy* is inept
for New discoveries ; and therefore
of no accommodation to the *use* of *life.*
That all Arts, and Professions are capable
of mature improvements ; cannot be doubted
by those, who know the least of any. And
that there is an *America* of secrets, and
unknown *Peru* of Nature, whose discovery

would richly advance them, is more then conjecture. Now while we either sayl by the *Land* of gross and vulgar Doctrines, or direct our Enquiries by the *Cynosure* of meer abstract *notions* ; we are not likely to reach the Treasures on the other side the *Atlantick* : The directing of the World the way to which, is the noble end of true *Philosophy.* That the *Aristotelian Physiology* cannot boast it self the proper Author of any one Invention ; is prægnant evidence of its infecundous deficiency : And 'twould puzzle the Schools to point at any consideable discovery, made by the direct, sole manuduction of *Peripatetick* Principles. Most of our Rarities have been found out by *casual emergency* ; and have been the works of Time, and Chance, rather then of *Philosophy.* What *Aristotle* hath of Experimental Knowledge in his Books of *Animals,* or else-where ; is not much transcending vulgar observation : And yet what he hath of this, was never learnt from his *Hypotheses* ; but forcibly fetch'd in to suffrage to them. And 'tis the observation of the Noble St. *Alban* ; that that *Philosophy* is built on a few Vulgar experiments : and if upon further enquiry, any were found to

refragate, they were to be discharg'd by a
distinction. Now what is founded on, and
made up but of *Vulgarities,* cannot make
known any thing beyond them. For Nature
is set a going by the most *subtil* and *hidden*
Instruments ; which it may be have nothing
obvious which resembles them. Hence
judging by visible appearances, we are
discouraged by supposed *Impossibilities*
which to *Nature* are none, but within her
Sphear of Action. And therefore what
shews only the outside, and sensible structure of Nature ; is not likely to help us in
finding out the *Magnalia.* 'Twere next to
impossible for one, who never saw the
inward wheels and motions, to make a
watch upon the bare view of the *Circle* of
hours, and *Index*: And 'tis as difficult to
trace natural operations to any practical
advantage, by the sight of the *Cortex* of
sensible Appearances. He were a poor
Physitian, that had no more *Anatomy,* then
were to be gather'd from the *Physnomy.*
Yea, the most common *Phænomena* can be
neither known, nor improved, without insight
into the more *hidden* frame. For *Nature*
works by an *Invisible Hand* in all things :
And till *Peripateticism* can shew us further,

then those gross solutions of *Qualities* and
Elements ; 'twill never make us Benefactors
to the World, nor considerable Discoverers.
But its experienc'd sterility through so many
hundred years, drives hope to desperation.

We expect greater things from *Neoterick*
endeavours. The *Cartesian Philosophy* in
this regard hath shewn the World the way
to be happy.   And me thinks this Age
seems resolved to bequeath *posterity* somewhat to remember it : The glorious Undertakers, wherewith Heaven hath blest our
dayes, will leave the world better provided
then they found it.   And whereas in former
times such generous free-spirited Worthies
were as the Rare newly observed *Stars*, a
single one the wonder of an Age : In ours
they are like the lights of the greater size
that twinkle in the *Starry Firmament* : And
this last Century can glory in numerous
constellations.   Should those *Heroes* go on,
as they have happily begun, they'll fill the
world with *wonders*.   And I doubt not but
posterity will find many things, that are now
but *Rumors*, verified into *practical Realities*.
It may be some Ages hence, a voyage to
the *Southern* unknown *Tracts*, yea possibly
the *Moon*, will not be more strange then one

to *America.* To them, that come after us, it may be as ordinary to buy a *pair* of *wings* to fly into remotest *Regions* ; as now a *pair* of *Boots* to ride a *Journey.* And to confer at the distance of the *Indies* by *Sympathetick* conveyances, may be as usual to future times, as to us in a *litterary* correspondence. The *restauration* of gray hairs to *Juvenility,* and renewing the exhausted marrow, may at length be effected without a *miracle* : And the turning of the now comparative *desert* world into a *Paradise,* may not improbably be expected from late *Agriculture.*

Now those, that judge by the narrowness of former *Principles* and *Successes,* will smile at these *Paradoxical expectations* : But questionless those great Inventions, that have in these later Ages altered the face of all things ; in their naked proposals, and meer suppositions, were to former times as *ridiculous.* To have talk'd of a *new Earth* to have been discovered, had been a *Romance* to *Antiquity* : And to sayl without sight of *Stars* or *shoars* by the guidance of a *Mineral,* a *story* more absurd then the flight of *Dædalus.* That men should speak after their *tongues* were *ashes,* or communicate with each other in differing *Hemisphears*, before the Invention of *Letters*; could not but have been thought a *fiction*. *Antiquity* would not have believed the almost incredible force of our *Canons*; and would as coldly have entertain'd the wonders of the Telescope. In these we all condemn *antique incredulity*; and 'tis likely Posterity will have as much cause to pity *ours*. But yet notwithstanding this straightness of shallow observers, there are a set of enlarged souls that are more *judiciously credulous*: and those, who are acquainted with the fecundity of *Cartesian Principles*, and the diligent and ingenious endeavours of so many true *Philosophers*; will despair of nothing.

CHAP. XXII.

(5.) *The* Aristotelian Philosophy *inconsistent with* Divinity ; *and* (6.) *with it self. The Conclusion of the* Reflexions.

BUT again (5.) the *Aristotelian Philosophy* is in some things *impious*, and *inconsistent* with *Divinity*. That the *Resur-*

rection is impossible : That *God* understands
not all things : That the *world* was from
Eternity : That there's no *substantial form*,
but moves some *Orb* : That the first Mover
moves by an *Eternal, Immutable Necessity :*
That, if the world and motion were not
from Eternity, then *God* was Idle : were all
the Assertions of *Aristotle*, and such as
Theology pronounceth impieties. Which
yet we need not strange at from one, of
whom a *Father* saith, *Nec Deum coluit nec
curavit* : Especially, if it be as *Philoponus*
affirms, that he *philosophiz'd* by command
from the *Oracle.* But besides those I have
mention'd, I might present to view a larger
Catalogue of *Aristotle's* Impious opinions ;
of which take a few :

He makes one *God* the *First Mover*, but
56 others, movers of the *Orbs.* He calls
God an *Animal* : and affirms, that He
knows not *particulars.* He denies that *God*
made any thing, or can do any thing but
move the *Heavens.* He affirms, that 'tis
not *God* but *Nature, Chance,* and *Fortune*
that rule the *World.* That he is tyed to
the *first Orb* ; and *preserves* not the World,
but only *moves* the *Heavens* ; and yet else-
where, that the World and Heavens have

infinite power to move themselves. He affirms, the *Soul* cannot be *separated* from the *Body*, because 'tis it's *Form.* That *Prayers* are to no purpose, because God understands not particulars. That God hears no *Prayers*, nor loves any man. That the *Soul perisheth* with the *body* : And that there is neither *state*, nor *place* of Happiness after this life is ended. All which *Dogmata*, how contrary they are to the Fundamental Principles of *Reason* and *Religion*, is easily determin'd : and perhaps, never did any worse drop from the Pens of the most vile contemners of the Deity. So that the Great and most Learned *Origen*, was not unjust in præferring *Epicurus* before the adored *Stagyrite.* And possibly there have been few men in the world have deserv'd less of *Religion*, and those that profess it. How it is come about then, that the Assertour of such *impieties*, should be such an Oracle among *Divines* and *Christians* ; is I confess to me, matter of some astonishment. And how *Epicurus* became so infamous, when *Aristotle* who spake as *ill*, and did *worse*, hath been so *sacred*, may well be wondred at.

AGAIN (6.) The *Peripatetick Philosophy* is repugnant to it *Self*; as also it was contrary to the more *antient Wisdom.* And therefore the learned *Patritius* saith of *Aristotle, Ob eam rem multos è patribus habuit oppugnatores, celebratorem neminem.* And within the same period of sense affirms, *Ipse sibi ipsi non constat*; *immo sæpissimè, immo semper secum pugnat.* Of the *Aristotelian contradictions, Gassendus* hath presented us with a Catalogue: We'll instance in a few of them. In one place he saith, The *Planets scintillation* is not seen, because of their *propinquity*; but that of the *rising* and *setting Sun* is, because of its *distance*: and yet in another place he makes the *Sun* nearer us, then they are. He saith, that the *Elements* are not *Eternal*, and seeks to prove it; and yet he makes the *world so*, and the *Elements* its parts. In his *Meteors* he saith, no Dew is produced in the Wind; and yet afterwards admits it under the *South*, and none under the *North.* In one place he defines a vapour *humid* and *cold*; and in another *humid* and *hot.* He saith, the *faculty* of speaking is a *sense*; and yet before he allow'd but *five.* In one place, that Nature doth all things *best*; and

L

in another, that it makes more *evil* then *good*. And somewhere he contradicts himself within a *line* ; saying, that an *Immoveable Mover* hath no principle of *Motion.* 'Twould be tedious to mention more ; and the quality of a *digression* will not allow it.

Thus we have, as briefly as the subject would bear, animadverted on the so much admired *Philosophy* of *Aristotle.* The nobler Spirits of the Age, are disengaged from those detected vanities : And the now Adorers of that *Philosophy* are few, but such as know no other : Or if any of them look beyond the leaves of their *Master*, yet they try other Principles by a Jury of his, and scan *Des-Cartes* by *Genus* and *Species.* From the former sort I may hope, they'l pardon this attempt ; since nothing but the Authors weakness hindred his obliging them. And for the latter, I value not their censure.

WE may conclude upon the whole then, that the stamp of *Authority* can make *Leather* as current as *Gold* ; and that there's nothing so *contemptible*, but *Antiquity* can render it *august*, and *excellent.* But, because the Fooleries of some affected Novelists have discredited new discoveries, and render'd the very mention suspected of *Vanity* at least ; and in points Divine, of *Heresie* : It will be necessary to add, that I intend not the former discourse, in favour of any new-broach'd conceit in *Divinity* : For I own no Opinion there, which cannot plead the pre-scription of above *sixteen hundred.* There's nothing I have more sadly resented, then the crasie whimsies with which our Age abounds, and therefore am not likely to Patron them. In *Theology,* I put as great a difference between our *New Lights*, and *Antient Truths*, as between the *Sun*, and an unconcocted evanid *Meteor.* Though I confess, that in *Philosophy* I'm a *Seeker*; yet cannot believe that a *Sceptick* in *Philosophy* must be one in *Divinity.* *Gospel-light* began in its *Zenith*; and, as some say the *Sun*, was created in its *Meridian* strength and lustre. But the beginnings of *Philosophy* were in a *Crepus-culous obscurity* ; and It's not yet scarce past the *Dawn.* *Divine* Truths were most pure in their source ; and *Time* could not perfect what *Eternity* began : our *Divinity*, like the Grand-father of *Humanity*, was born in the *fulness* of *time*, and in the strength of its manly vigour: But *Philosophy* and Arts commenced *Embryo's*, and are by

L 2

Times gradual accomplishments. And therefore, what I cannot find in the leaves of former Inquisitours : I seek in the Modern attempts of nearer Authors.   I cannot receive *Aristotle's* ΠΙΣΤΟΤΑΤΟΙ ΠΑΛΑΙΟΙ, in so extensive an interpretation, as some would enlarge it to : And that discouraging Maxime, *Nil dictum quod non dictum prius,* hath little *room* in my *estimation.* Nor can I tye up my belief to the *Letter* of *Solomon* : Except *Copernicus* be in the right, there hath been something *New under* the *Sun* ; I'm sure, later times have seen *Novelties* in the Heavens *above* it.   I do not think, that all Science is *Tautology* :   The last Ages have shewn us, what *Antiquity* never saw ; no not in a *Dream.*

CHAP. XXIII.

It's queried whether there be any Science in the sense of the Dogmatists : (1.) We cannot know any thing to be the cause of another, but from its attending it; and this way is not infallible; declared by instances, especially from the Philosophy of Des-Cartes. *All things are mixt; and 'tis difficult to assign each Cause its distinct Effects.* (2.) *There's no demonstration but where the contrary is impossible. And we can scarce conclude so of any thing.*

CONFIDENCE of *Science* is one great reason, we miss it : For on this account presuming we have it every where, we seek it not where it is ; and therefore fall short of the object of our Enquiry. Now to give further check to *Dogmatical* pretensions, and to discover the vanity of assuming *Ignorance* ; we'll make a short enquiry, whether there be any such thing as *Science* in the sense of its Assertours. In their notion then, *It is the knowledge of things in their true, immediate, necessary* causes: Upon which I'le advance the following Observations.

1. All Knowledge of Causes is *deductive* : for we know none by simple intuition ; but through the mediation of their effects. So that we cannot conclude, any thing to be the cause of another ; but from its continual accompanying it : for the *causality* it self is *insensible.* But now to argue from a concomitancy to a causality, is not infallibly conclusive : Yea in this way lies notorious delusion. For suppose, for instance, we had never seen more *Sun,* then in a cloudy day ; and that the lesser lights had ne're appeared : Let us suppose the *day* had alway broke with a *wind,* and had proportionably varyed, as *that* did : Had not he been a notorious *Sceptick,* that should question the causality? But we need not be beholding to so remote a supposition : The French *Philosophy* furnishes us with a better instance. For, according to the Principles of the illustrious *Des-Cartes,* there would be *light,* though the Sun and Stars gave *none* ; and a great part of what we now enjoy, is

independent on their beams. Now if this seemingly prodigious *Paradox*, can be reconcil'd to the least probability of conjecture, or may it be made but a tolerable supposal ; I presume, it may then win those that are of most difficult belief, readily to yield, that causes in our account the most palpable, may possibly be but *uninfluential attendants* ; since that there is not an instance can be given, wherein we opinion a more certain *efficiency*. So then, according to the tenour of that concinnous *Hypothesis*, light being caused by the *Conamen* of the Matter of the *Vortex*, to recede from the Centre of its Motion : it is an easie inference, that were there none of that fluid *Æther*, which makes the body of the Sun in the Centre of our world, or should it cease from action ; yet the *conatus* of the circling matter would not be considerably less, but according to the indispensable Laws of Motion, must press the Organs of Sense as now ; though it may be, not with so smart an impulse. Thus we see, how there might be *Light* before the *Luminaries* ; and *Evening* and *Morning* before there was a *Sun*. So then we cannot infallibly assure our selves of the truth of the *causes*, that most obviously occur ; and

therefore the foundation of *scientifical* procedure, is too weak for so magnificent a
superstructure.

Besides, That the World's a mass of
heterogeneous subsistencies, and every part
thereof a coalition of distinguishable varie-
ties ; we need not go far for evidence : And
that all things are *mixed*, and Causes blended
by mutual involutions ; I presume, to the
Intelligent will be no difficult concession.
Now to profound to the bottom of these
diversities, to assign each cause its distinct
effects, and to limit them by their *just* and
true proportions ; are necessary requisites of
Science : and he that hath compast them,
may boast he hath out-done *humanity.*   But
for us to talk of *Knowledge*, from those few
indistinct representations, which are made to
our grosser faculties, is a *flatulent vanity.*

2. We hold no *demonstration* in the notion
of the *Dogmatist*, but where the contrary is
impossible : For *necessary is that, which
cannot be other wise.* Now, whether the
acquisitions of any on this side perfection,
can make good the pretensions to so high
strain'd an *infallibility*, will be worth a
reflexion. And methinks, did we but compare the miserable *scantness* of our *capacities,*

with the vast *profoundity* of *things*; both truth and modesty would teach us a more wary and becoming language. Can nothing be otherwise, which we conceive *impossible* to be so? Is our knowledge, so adequately commensurate with the nature of things, as to justifie such an affirmation, that that cannot be, which we comprehend not? Our demonstrations are levyed upon Principles of our *own*, not *universal Nature* : And, as my Lord *Bacon* notes, we judge from the *Analogy* of *our selves*, not the *Universe*. Now are not many things *certain* by one man's *Principles*, which are *impossible* to the apprehensions of another? Some things our Juvenile reasons tenaciously adhere to ; which yet our maturer Judgements disallow of : And that to meer sensible discerners is *impossible*, which to the enlarged principles of more advanced *Intellects* is an easie variety : Yea, that's absurd in one *Philo-sophy*, which is a worthy Truth in another ; and that is a demonstration to *Aristotle*, which is none to *Des-Cartes*. That every fixt *star* is a *Sun*; and that they are as distant from each other, as we from some of them : That the *Sun*, which lights us, is in the *Centre* of our World, and our *Earth* a *Planet* that wheels about it : That this *Globe* is a *Star*, only crusted over with the grosser Element, and that its *Centre* is of the same nature with the *Sun* : That it may recover its light again, and shine amids the other *Luminaries*: That our *Sun* may be swallow'd up of another, and become a *Planet* : All these, if we judge by common Principles, or the Rules of Vulgar *Philosophy*, are prodigious *Impossibilities*, and their contradictories, as good as *demonstrable* : But yet to a reason inform'd by *Cartesianism*, these have their probability. Thus, it may be, the grossest absurdities to the Philosophies of *Europe*, may be justifiable assertions to that of *China* : And tis not unlikely, but what's impossible to all *Humanity*, may be possible in the *Metaphysicks*, and *Physiologie* of Angels. For the best Principles, excepting *Divine*, and *Mathematical*, are but *Hypotheses* ; within the Circle of which, we may indeed conclude many things, with security from Error : But yet the greatest certainty, advanc'd from supposal, is still but *Hypothetical.* So that we may affirm, that things are thus and thus, according to the *Principles* we have espoused : But we strangely forget our selves, when we plead a necessity of their being so in *Nature*, and an Impossibility of their being otherwise.

CHAP. XXIV.

Three Instances of reputed Impossibilities, *which likely are not so, as* (1.) *of the power of* Imagination. (2.) Secret Conveyance. (3.) Sympathetick Cures.

NOW to shew how rashly we use to conclude things *impossible* ; I'le instance in some reputed *Impossibilities*, which are only strange and difficult performances. And the Instances are Three : (1.) The power of one man's imagination upon anothers. (2.) *Momentous* conveyance at almost any distance. (3.) *Sympathetick Cures.*

(1) That the *Phancy* of one Man should *bind* the Thoughts of another, and determine them to their particular objects, will be thought *impossible* : which yet, if we look deeply into the matter, wants not it's probability. The judicious Naturalist my Lord

Bacon, speaks not unfavourably of this way of *secret influence* : And that the spirit of one man hath sometimes a power over that of another, I think is well attested by experience. For some presences daunt and discourage us, when others raise us to a brisk assurance. And I believe there are few but find that some Companies benumb and cramp them, so that in them they can neither speak nor do any thing that is handsom : whereas among more congruous and suitable tempers they find themselves very lucky and fortunate both in Speech and Action. Which things seem to me pretty considerable evidence of immaterial intercourses between our Spirits. And that this kind of secret influence may be advanc't to so strange an operation in the Imagination of one upon another, as to fix and determine it. Methinks the wonderful *signatures* of the *Fœtus* caused by the Imagination of the Mother, is no contemptible Item. The *sympathies* of laughing and gaping together, are resolv'd into this Principle : and I see not why the *phancy* of one man may not determine the cogitation of another rightly qualified, as easily as his *bodily motion.* Nor doth this influence seem more unreasonable, then that of one *string* of a Lute upon another, when a *stroak* on it causeth a proportionable motion in the *sympathizing* consort, which is distant from it and not sensibly touched. And if there be truth in this notion ; 'twill yield us a good account how *Angels* inject thoughts into our minds, and know our cogitations : and here we may see the source of some kinds of *fascination.*

Now, though in our inquiry after the Reason of this operation, we can receive no assistance from the common *Philosophy* ; yet the *Platonical Hypothesis* of a *Mundane Soul* will handsomely relieve us. Or if any would rather have a *Mechanical* account ; I think it may probably be made out some such way as follows. *Imagination* is inward Sense ; To *Sense* is required a motion of certain *Filaments* of the Brain ; and consequently in *Imagination* there's the like : they only differing in this, that the motion of the one proceeds immediately from external objects; but that of the other hath its immediate rise within our selves. Now then, when any part of the Brain is strongly agitated; that which is next and most capable to receive the *motive* Impress, must in like man-

ner be moved. And we cannot conceive any
thing more capable of motion, then the
fluid matter, that's interspers'd among all
bodies, and contiguous to them. So then,
the agitated pars of the Brain begetting a
motion in the proxime *Æther* ; it is propagated through the liquid *medium* ; as we
see the motion is which is caus'd by a stone
thrown into the water. And when the thus
moved *matter* meets with any thing like
that, from which it received its primary
impress ; it will in like manner move it ;
as it is in *Musical strings* tuned *Unisons.*
And thus the motion being convey'd, from
the *Brain* of one man to the *Phancy* of
another ; it is there receiv'd from the instrument of conveyance, the *subtil* matter ;
and the same kind of *strings* being moved,
and much what after the same manner as in
the first *Imaginant* ; the *Soul* is awaken'd
to the same apprehensions, as were they that
caus'd them. I pretend not to any exactness
or infallibility in this account, fore-seeing
many scruples that must be removed to
make it perfect : 'Tis only an hint of the
possibility of mechanically solving the *Phæ-
nomenon* ; though very likely it may require
many other circumstances compleatly to

make it out. But 'tis not my business here to follow it : I leave it therefore to receive accomplishment from maturer Inventions.

But (2.) to advance another instance. That Men should confer at very distant removes by an *extemporary* intercourse, is another reputed *impossibility* ; but yet there are some hints in Natural operations, that give us probability that it is feasible, and may be compast without unwarrantable correspondence with the people of the Air. That a couple of *Needles* equally touched by the same *magnet*, being set in two Dyals exactly proportion'd to each other, and circumscribed by the Letters of the *Alphabet*, may effect this *Magnale*, hath considerable authorities to avouch it. The manner of it is thus represented. Let the friends that would communicate, take each a Dyal : and having appointed a time for their *Sympathetick* conference, let one move his impregnate *Needle* to any letter in the *Alphabet*, and its affected fellow will precisely respect the same. So that would I know what my friend would acquaint me with ; 'tis but observing the letters that are pointed at by my *Needle*, and in their order transcribing them from their *sympathizing Index*, as its motion direct's : and I may be assured that my friend described the same with his : and that the words on my paper, are of his inditing.   Now though there will be some ill contrivance in a circumstance of this invention, in that the thus *impregnate Needles* will not move to, but avert from each other (as ingenious Dr. *Browne* in his *Pseudodoxia Epidemica* hath observed :) yet this cannot prejudice the main design of this way of secret conveyance : Since 'tis˙ but reading counter to the *magnetick* informer ; and noting the letter which is most distant in the *Abecedarian circle* from that which the Needle turns to, and the case is not alter'd. Now though this pretty contrivance possibly may not yet answer the expectation of inquisitive *experiment* ; yet 'tis no despicable item, that by some other such way of *magnetick efficiency*, it may hereafter with success be attempted, when *Magical* History shall be enlarged by riper inspections : and 'tis not unlikely, but that present discoveries might be improved to the performance.

Besides this there is another way of secret conveyance that's whisper'd about the World, the *truth* of which I vouch not, but the *possibility* : it is conference at distance by sympathized handes. For say the relatours of this strange secret : The hands of two friends being allyed by the transferring of *Flesh* from one into another, and the place of the Letters mutually agreed on ; the least prick in the hand of one, the other will be sensible of, and that in the same part of his own. And thus the distant friend, by a new kind of *Chiromancy,* may read in his own hand what his correspondent had set down in his. For instance, would I in *London* acquaint my intimate in *Paris,* that *I am well* : I would then prick that part where I had appointed the letter [*I* :] and doing so in another place to signifie that word was done, proceed to [*A,*] thence to [*M*] and so on, till I had finisht what I intended to make known.

Now if these seemingly prodigious Phancies of secret conveyances prove to be but *possible,* they will be warrantable presumption of the verity of the former instance : since tis as easily conceivable, that there should be communications between the *phancies* of men, as either the *impregnate needles,* or *sympathized hands.*

M

And there is an instance still behind, which is more credible than either, and gives probability to them all.

(3.) Then there is a *Magnetick* way of curing *wounds* by anointing the *weapon*, and that the wound is affected in like manner as is the *extravenate blood* by the *Sympathetick medicine*, as to matter of fact is with circumstances of good evidence asserted by the Noble Sir *K. Digby* in his ingenious discourse on the subject. The reason of this *magnale* he attempts by *Mechanism*, and endeavours to make it out by *atomical aporrheas*, which passing from the *cruentate* cloth or weapon to the wound, and being incorporated with the *particles* of the *salve* carry them in their embraces to the affected part : where the *medicinal atomes* entering together with the *effluviums* of the blood, do by their subtle insinuation better effect the cure, then can be done by any grosser Application. The particular way of their conveyance, and their regular direction is handsomely explicated by that learned *Knight*, and recommended to the Ingenious by most witty and becoming illustrations. It is out of my way here to enquire whether the *Anima Mundi* be not a better account, then any *Mechanical* Solutions. The former is more desperate ; the latter perhaps hath more of ingenuity, then good ground of satisfaction. It is enough for me that *de facto* there is such an intercourse between the *Magnetick unguent* and the *vulnerated* body, and I need not be solicitous of the Cause. These *Theories* I presume will not be importunate to the ingenious : and therefore I have taken the liberty (which the quality of a Essay will well enough allow of) to touch upon them, though seemingly collateral to my scope. And yet I think, they are but seemingly so, since they do pertinently illustrate my design, *viz.* That what seems *impossible* to *us*, may not be so in *Nature* ; and therefore the *Dogmatist* wants this to compleat his demonstration, that '*tis impossible to be otherwise.*

Now I intend not any thing here to invalidate the certainty of truths either *Mathematical* or *Divine.* These are superstructed on principles that cannot fail us, except our faculties do constantly abuse us. Our *religious foundations* are fastened at the pillars of the *intellectual* world, and the grand *Articles* of our Belief as demonstrable as *Geometry.* Nor will ever either the subtile attempts of the resolved *Atheist,* or the passionate Hurricanoes of the wild *Enthusiast,* any more be able to prevail against the *reason* our *Faith* is built on, than the blustring *winds* to blow out the *Sun.* And for *Mathematical Sciences,* he that doubts their certainty, hath need of a dose of *Hellebore.* Nor yet can the *Dogmatist* make much of these concessions in favour of his pretended *Science*; for our discourse comes not within the circle of the former : and for the later, the knowledge we have of the *Mathematicks,* hath no reason to elate us ; since by them we know but *numbers,* and *figures,* creatures of our own, and are yet ignorant of our *Maker's.*

(3.) We cannot know any thing in Nature without knowing the first springs of Natural Motions; and these we are ignorant of. (4.) Causes are so connected that we cannot know any without knowing all; declared by Instances.

BUT (3.) we cannot know any thing of *Nature* but by an *Analysis* of it to its *true initial causes* : and till we know the first springs of natural motions, we are still but Ignorants. These are the *Alphabet* of Science, and Nature cannot be *read* without them. Now who dares pretend to have seen the *prime motive causes*, or to have had a view of *Nature*, while she lay in her *simple Originals?* we know nothing but *effects*, and those but by our *Senses.* Nor can we judge of their *Causes*, but by proportion to palpable causalities, conceiving them like those within the sensible *Horizon.* Now t'is no doubt with the considerate, but that the *rudiments* of

Nature are very unlike the grosser *appearances*. Thus in things obvious, there's but little resemblance between the *Mucous sperm*, and the compleated *Animal*. The *Egge* is not like the *oviparous* production : nor the corrupted *muck* like the *creature* that creeps from it. There's but little similitude betwixt a *terreous humidity*, and *plantal* germinations ; nor do *vegetable* derivations ordinarily resemble their *simple seminalities*. So then, since there's so much dissimilitude between *Cause* and *Effect* in the more palpable *Phænomena*, we can expect no less between them, and their *invisible* efficients. Now had our Senses never presented us with those obvious *seminal* principles of apparent generations, we should never have suspected that a *plant* or *animal* could have proceeded from such unlikely *materials* : much less, can we conceive or determine the uncompounded *initials* of natural productions, in the total silence of our Senses. And though the Grand Secretary of Nature, the miraculous *Des-Cartes* hath here infinitely out-done all the Philosophers that went before him, in giving a particular and *Analytical* account of the *Universal Fabrick* : yet he intends his Principles but for *Hy-pothises*, and never pretends that things are really or necessarily, as he hath supposed them : but that they may be admitted pertinently to solve the *Phænomena*, and are convenient supposals for the *use of life*. Nor can any further account be expected from humanity, but how things possibly *may have been made* consonantly to sensible nature : but infallibly to determine how *they truly were effected*, is proper to him only that saw them in the *Chaos*, and fashion'd them out of that confused *mass*. For to say, the *principles* of Nature must needs be such as our *Philosophy* makes them, is to set bounds to *Omnipotence*, and to confine *infinite power* and *wisdom* to our shallow *models*.

(4.) According to the notion of the *Dog-matist*, we *know nothing*, except we *knew all things* ; and he that pretends to *Science* affects an *Omniscience*. For all things being linkt together by an uninterrupted *chain* of *Causes* ; and every single motion owning a dependence on such a *Syndrome* of præ-required *motors* : we can have no true knowledge of any, except we comprehend all,

and could distinctly pry into the whole
method of *Causal Concatenations*. Thus we
cannot *know* the cause of any one *motion*
in a *watch*, unless we were acquainted with
all its motive dependences, and had a distinctive comprehension of the whole
Mechanical frame. And would we *know*
but the most contemptible *plant* that grows,
almost all things that have a being, must
contribute to our *knowledge* : for, that to
the perfect *Science* of any thing it's necessary
to know all its *causes* ; is both reasonable in
its self, and the sense of the *Dogmatist.*
So that, to the knowledge of the poorest
simple, we must first know its *efficient*, the
manner, and *method* of its *efformation*, and
the nature of the *Plastick*. To the com-
prehending of which, we must have a full
prospect into the whole *Archidoxis* of
Nature's secrets, and the immense profundi-
ties of *occult* Philosophy : in which we
know nothing till we compleatly ken all
Magnetick, and *Sympathetick* energies, and
their most hidden causes. And (2.) if we
contemplate a *vegetable* in its *material* principle, and look on it as made of *Earth* ; we
must have the true Theory of the nature
of that Element, or we miserably fail of

our *Scientifical* aspirings, and while we can only say, 'tis *cold* and *dry*, we are pitiful *knowers*. But now, to profound into the *Physicks* of this heterogeneous mass, to discern the principles of its constitution, and to discover the reason of its diversities, are absolute requisites of the *Science* we aim at. Nor can we tolerably pretend to have those without the knowledge of *Minerals*, the *causes* and *manner* of their Concretions, and among the rest, the *Magnet*, with its amazing properties. This directs us to the *pole*, and thence our disquisition is led to the whole *systeme* of the *Heavens* : to the knowledge of which, we must know their *motions*, and the *causes*, and *manner* of their *rotations*, as also the reasons of all the *Planetary Phænomena*, and of the *Comets*, their *nature*, and the *causes* of all their *irregular appearings*. To these, the knowledge of the intricate doctrine of *motion*, the *powers*, *proportions*, and *laws* thereof, is requisite. And thus we are engaged in the objects of *Geometry* and *Arithmetick* ; yea the whole *Mathematicks*, must be contributary, and to them all *Nature* payes a subsidy. Besides, *plants* are partly material'd of *water*, with which they are furnisht either from *subterranean* Fountains, or the *Clouds.* Now to have the true Theory of the former, we must trace the nature of the *Sea*, its origen ; and hereto its remarkable *motions* of *flux* and *reflux.* This again directs us to the *Moon*, and the rest of the Celestial *phaseis.* The moisture that comes from the *Clouds* is drawn up in *vapours* : To the Scientifical discernment of which, we must know the *nature* and *manner* of that action, their suspense in the *middle region*, the qualities of that *place*, and the *causes* and *manner* of their precipitating thence again : and so the reason of the *Sphærical* figure of the *drops* ; the causes of *Windes, Hail, Snow, Thunder, Lightning*, with all other igneous appearances, with the whole *Physiology* of *Meteors* must be enquired into. And again (3.) in our disquisition into the *formal Causes*, the knowledge of the nature of *colours*, is necessary to compleat the Science. To be inform'd of this, we must know what *light* is ; and *light* being effected by a motion on the Organs of *sense*, 'twill be a necessary requisite, to understand the nature of our *sensitive* faculties, and to them the essence of the *soul*, and other spiritual subsistences. The manner how it is *materially* united, and how it is aware of corporeal *motion*. The seat of *sense*, and the place where 'tis *principally* affected : which cannot be known but by the *Anatomy* of our parts, and the knowledge of their Mechanical structure. And if further (4.) we contemplate the *end* of the *effect* we instanc't in, its *principal final* Cause, being the *glory* of its *Maker*, leads us into *Divinity* ; and for its *subordinate*, as 'tis design'd for *alimental* sustenance to living creatures, and *medicinal* uses to man, we are conducted into *Zoography*, and the whole body of *Physick*. Thus then, to the *knowledge* of the most contemptible *effect* in nature, 'tis necessary to know the whole *Syntax* of Causes, and their particular *circumstances*, and *modes* of action. Nay, we *know nothing*, till we *know our selves*, which are the summary of all the world without us, and the *Index* of the Creation. Nor can we know our selves without the *Physiology* of corporeal Nature, and the *Metaphysicks* of Souls and Angels. So then, every Science borrows from all the rest ; and we cannot attain any single one, without the *Encyclopædy*. I have been the more diffuse and particular upon this head, because it affordes a catalogue of the Instances of our *Ignorance* ; and therefore though it may seem too largely spoken to in relation to the particular I am treating of, yet 'tis not improper in a more general reference to the subject.

C H A P.   X X V I.

All our Science *comes in at our* senses. *Their* infallibility *inquired into. The Authors design in this last particular.*

THE *knowledge* we have comes from our *senses*, and the *Dogmatist* can go no higher for the original of his certainty. Now let the *Sciolist* tell me, why things must needs be *so*, as his individual *senses* represent them. Is he sure, that objects are not otherwise *sensed* by others, then they are by him? and why must his *sense* be the infallible *Criterion?* It may be, what is *white* to us, is *black* to *Negroes*, and our *Angels* to them are *Fiends*. Diversity of *constitution*, or other circumstances varies the *sensation*, and to them of *Java* Pepper is *cold*. And though we agree in a common name, yet it may be, I have the same representation from *yellow*, that another hath from *green*. Thus two look upon an *Alabaster* Statue ; he call's it *white*, and I assent to the appellation : but how can I discover, that his inward *sense* on't is the same that mine is? It may be *Alabaster* is represented to him, as *Jet* is to me, and yet it is *white* to us both. We accord in the *name* : but it's beyond our knowledge, whether we do so in the *conception* answering it. Yea, the contrary is not without its probability. For though the *Images*, *Motions*, or whatever else is the cause of *sense*, may be alike as from the object ; yet may the representations be varyed according to the nature and quality of the Recipient. That's one thing to us looking through a *tube*, which is another to our naked *eyes*. The same things seem otherwise through a *green* glass, then they do through a *red*. Thus objects have a different appearance, when the *eye* is violently any way *distorted*, from that they have, when our Organs are in their proper *site* and *figure*, and some extraordinary alterations in the Brain duplicate that

which is but a single object to our undis-
temper'd *Sentient.* Thus, that's of one
colour to us standing in *one place*, which
hath a contrary aspect in *another*: as in
those versatile representations in the neck of
a *Dove*, and folds of *Scarlet.* And as great
diversity might have been exemplified in
the other *senses*, but for brevity I omit them.
Now then, since so many various circumstances concurre to every *individual* constitution, and every mans *senses*, differing as
much from others in its *figure, colour, site*,
and infinite other *particularities* in the
Organization, as any one mans can from it
self, through divers *accidental* variations: it
cannot well be suppos'd otherwise, but that
the *conceptions* convey'd by them must be as
diverse. Thus, one mans *eyes* are more
protuberant, and swelling out; anothers
more *sunk* and *depressed.* One mans *bright*,
and sparkling, and as it were swimming in a
subtile, lucid moisture; anothers more *dull*
and heavy, and destitute of that *spirituous*
humidity. The *colour* of mens *eyes* is
various, nor is there less diversity in their
bigness. And if we look further into the
more *inward* constitution, there's more
variety in the internal *configurations*, then in

the *visible* outside. For let us consider the different qualities of the *Optick* nerves, *humours*, *tumours* and spirits ; the divers *figurings* of the brain ; the *strings*, or *filaments* thereof ; their difference in tenuity and aptness for motion : and as many other circumstances, as there are individuals in *humane nature* ; all these are diversified according to the difference of each *Crasis*, and are as unlike, as our *faces*. From these diversities in all likelyhood will arise as much difference in the manner of the reception of the *Images*, and consequently as various *sensations*. So then, how objects are represented to my *self*, I cannot be ignorant, being conscious to mine own *cogitations* ; but in what manner they are received, and what impresses they make upon the so differing *organs* of another, he only *knows*, that *feels* them.

There is an obvious, an easie objection, which I have sufficiently caveated against ; and with the considerate it will signifie no more then the inadvertency of the Objectors. 'Twill be thought by sight discerners a ridiculous *Paradox*, that all men should not conceive of the objects of *sense* alike ; since their agreement in the *appellation* seems so strong an argument of the identity of the *sentiment*. All, for instance, say, that Snow is *white*, and that Jet is *black*, is doubted by none. But yet 'tis more then any man can determine, whether his *conceit* of what he calls *white*, be the same with anothers ; or whether, the notion he hath of one *colour* be not the same another hath of a very *diverse* one. So then, to direct all against the *knowing Ignorant*, what he hath of sensible evidence, the very ground work of his *demonstration*, is but the knowledge of his own *resentment* : but how the same things appear to others, they only *know*, that are *conscious* to them ; and how they are in *themselves* only he that *made them*.

Thus have I in this last particular play'd with the *Dogmatist* in a personated *Scepticism* : and would not have the design of the whole *discourse* measur'd by the seeming tendency of this part on't. The *Sciolist* may here see, that what he counts of all things most absurd and irrational, hath yet considerable shew of probability to plead its cause, and it may be more then some of his presumed *demonstrations*. 'Tis irreprehensible in *Physitians* to cure their Patient of one disease by casting him into another, less desperate. And I hope, I shall not deserve the frown of the Ingenuous for my innocent intentions ; having in this only imitated the practice of bending a *crooked* stick as much the other way, to straighten it. And if by this verge to the other extream, I can bring the *opinionative Confident* but half the way, *viz.* that discreet modest æquipoize of Judgment, that becomes the sons of *Adam* ; I have compast what I aim at.

C H A P.   X X V I I.

Considerations against Dogmatizing. (1.) *'Tis the effect of* Ignorance. (2.) *It inhabits with untamed* passions, *and an ungovern'd Spirit.* (3.) *It is the great* Disturber *of the World.* (4.) *It is* ill manners, *and immodesty.* (5.) *It holds men captive in* Error. (6.) *It betrayes a* narrowness *of* Spirit.

I EXPECT but little success of all this upon the *Dogmatist* ; his opinion'd assurance is paramont to Argument, and 'tis almost as easie to reason him out of a *Feaver*, as out of this *disease* of the mind. I hope for better

N

fruit from the more generous *Vertuosi*, to such I appeal against *Dogmatizing*, in the following considerations. That's well spent upon impartial ingenuity, which is lost upon resolved prejudice.

(1.) *Opinionative confidence* is the effect of *Ignorance*, and were the *Sciolist* perswaded *so*, I might spare my further reasons against it : 'tis affectation of *knowledge*, that makes him confident he hath *it* ; and his confidence is counter evidence to his pretensions to *knowledge*. He is the greatest *ignorant*, that knows not that he is *so* : for 'tis a good degree of *Science*, to be sensible that we *want it*. He that knows most of himself, knows least of his knowledge, and the exercised understanding is conscious of its disability. Now he that is so, will not lean too assuredly on that, which hath so frequently deceived him, nor build the *Castle* of his intellectual security, *in the Air of Opinions*. But for the shallow passive intellects, that were never engag'd in a thorough search of verity, 'tis such are the *confidents* that engage their irrepealable assents to every slight appearance. Thus meer sensible conceivers make every thing they hold a *Sacrament*, and

the silly vulgar are *sure* of all things   There
was no Theoreme in the *Mathematicks* more
certain to *Archimedes*, then the *Earth's* immoveable *quiescence* seems to the multitude :
nor then did the impossibility of *Antipodes*,
to antique ages. And if great *Philosophers*
doubt of many things, which popular dijudi-
cants hold as certain as their *Creeds*, I
suppose *Ignorance* it self will not say, it is
because they are more *ignorant.* Superficial
pedants will swear their controversal uncertainties, while wiser heads stand *in bivio.*
Opinions are the *Rattles* of immature intellects, but the advanced Reasons have out-
grown them.   True knowledge is modest
and wary ; 'tis ignorance that is so bold, and
presuming.   Thus those that never travail'd
beyond one *Horizon*, will not be perswaded
that the world hath any Countrey better then
their own : while they that have had a view
of other Regions, are not so confidently per
swaded of the precedency of that they were
bred in, but speak more indifferently of the
laws, manners, commodities, and *customs* of
their native soil : So they that never peep't
beyond the common belief in which their
easie understandings were at first indoctrin-
ated, are strongly assured of the Truth, and

comparative excellency of their receptions while the larger Souls, that have travelled the divers *Climates* of *Opinions*, are more cautious in their *resolves*, and more sparing to determine. And let the most confirm'd *Dogmatist* profound far into his indeared opinions, and I'le warrant him 'twill be an effectual cure of *confidence*.

(2.) *Confidence in Opinions* evermore dwells with untamed *passions*, and is maintained upon the depraved *obstinacy* of an ungovern'd *spirit*. He's but a novice in the Art of *Autocrasy*, that cannot castigate his *passions* in reference to those *presumptions*, and will come as far short of *wisdom* as *science* : for the Judgement being the leading power, and director of action, if It be swaid by the *over-bearings* of *passion*, and stor'd with *lubricous opinions* in stead of clearly conceived *truths*, and be peremptorily resolved in them, the *practice* will be as irregular, as the *conceptions* erroneous. *Opinions* hold the stirrup, while *vice* mount into the saddle.

(3.) *Dogmatizing* is the great disturber both of our *selves* and the *world* without us :

for while we wed an *opinion*, we resolvedly engage against every one that opposeth it. Thus *every man*, being in some of his *opinionative* apprehensions *singular*, must be at variance with *all men*. Now every opposition of our espous'd opinions furrows the *sea* within us, and discomposeth the minds *serenity*. And what happiness is there in a *storm* of passions? On this account the *Scepticks* affected an indifferent æquipondious *neutrality* as the only means to their *Ataraxia*, and freedom from *passionate* disturbances. Nor were they altogether mistaken in the way, to their design'd felicity, but came *short* on't, by going *beyond* it : for if there be a repose naturally attainable this side the *Stars*, there is no way we can more hopefully seek it in. We can never be at rest, while our quiet can be taken from us by every thwarting our opinions : nor is that content an happiness, which every one can rob us of. There is no *felicity*, but in a *fixed stability*. Nor can genuine *constancy* be built upon *rowling* foundations. 'Tis true staidness of mind, to look with an equal regard on all things ; and this unmoved *apathy* in opinionative uncertainties, is a warrantable piece of *Stoicism*.

Besides, this *immodest obstinacy* in opinions, hath made the world a *Babel* ; and given birth to disorders, like those of the *Chaos*. The primitive fight of *Elements* doth fitly embleme that of *Opinions*, and those *proverbial contrarieties* may be reconcil'd, as soon as peremptory contenders. That hence grow *Schisms, Heresies,* and *anomalies* beyond *Arithmetick*, I could wish were more difficult to be proved. 'Twere happy for a distemper'd *Church*, if evidence were not so near us. 'Tis zeal for *opinions* that hath filled our *Hemisphear* with smoke and darkness, and by a dear experience we know the fury of those *flames* it hath kindled. 'Tis lamentable that *Homo homini Dæmon*, should be a *Proverb* among the Professors of the *Cross* ; and yet I fear it is as verifiable among them, as of those without the pale of visible *Christianity*. I doubt we have lost S. *John's* sign of *regeneration : By this we know that we are past from death to life, that we love one another,* is I fear, to few a sign of their spiritual *resurrection*. If our Returning Lord, shall scarce find *faith* on earth, where will he look for *Charity* ? It is a stranger this side the Region of *love*, and *blessedness* ; bitter zeal for *opinions* hath

consum'd it. Mutual agreement and indear-
ments was the badge of *Primitive* Believers,
but we may be known by the contrary
criterion. The union of a Sect within it
self, is a pitiful *charity* : it's no concord of
Christians, but a conspiracy against *Christ* ;
and they that love one another, for their
opinionative concurrencies, love for their
own sakes, not their *Lords* : not because
they have his *image,* but because they bear
one *anothers.* What a stir is there for *Mint,*
Anise, and *Cummin controversies,* while the
great practical *fundamentals* are unstudyed,
unobserved? What eagerness in the prose-
cution of *disciplinarian* uncertainties, when
the *love* of God and our *neighbour,* those
Evangelical *unquestionables,* are neglected?
'Tis this hath consum'd the nutriment of the
great and more necessary Verities, and bred
differences that are past any accommodation,
but that of the *last dayes* decisions. The
sight of that day will resolve us, and make
us asham'd of our petty quarrels.

Thus *Opinions* have rent the world
asunder, and divided it almost into *in-*
divisibles. Had *Heraclitus* liv'd now, he
had wept himself into *marble,* and *Demo-*
critus would have broke his *spleen.* Who

can speak of such fooleries without a *Satyr*, to see aged Infants so quarrel at *putpin*, and the *doating* world grown child *again ?* How fond are men of a bundle of *opinions*, which are no better then a bagge of *Cherry-stones ?* How do they *scramble* for their *Nuts*, and *Apples*, and how zealous for their petty Victories? Methinks those grave contenders about *opinionative trifles*, look like aged *Socrates* upon his boyes *Hobby-horse*, or like something more *ludicrous* : since they make things their *seria*, which are scarce tolerable in their sportful *intervals*.

(4.) To be *confident in Opinions* is *ill manners* and *immodesty* ; and while we are peremptory in our perswasions, we accuse all of *Ignorance* and *Error*, that subscribe not our assertions. The *Dogmatist* gives the *lye* to all dissenting apprehenders, and proclaims his judgement fittest, to be the *Intellectual Standard.* This is that spirit of immorality, that saith unto dissenters, *Stand off*, I am more *Orthodox then thou art* : a vanity more capital then Error. And he that affirms that things must needs be as he apprehends them, implies that none can be right till they submit to his *opinions*, and take him for their director.

(5.) *Obstinacy in Opinions* holds the Dogmatist in the chains of *Error*, without hope of emancipation. While we are confident of *all* things, we are fatally deceiv'd in *most*. He that assures himself he never *erres*, will alwayes *erre* ; and his presumptions will render all attempts to inform him, ineffective. We use not to seek further for what we think we are possest of ; and when falshood is without suspicion embrac't in the stead of truth, and with confidence retained : *Verity* will be rejected as a supposed Error, and irreconcileably be hated, because it opposeth what is truly so.

(6.) It betrayes a *poverty* and *narrowness* of *spirit*, in the Dogmatical assertors. There are a set of Pedants that are born to slavery. But the more generous spirit preserves the liberty of his judgement, and will not pen it up in an *Opinionative Dungeon* ; with an equal respect he examins all things, and judgeth as impartially as *Rhadamanth* : When as the Pedant can hear nothing but in favour of the conceits he is amorous of ;

and cannot *see*, but out of the grates of his *prison* ; the determinations of the nobler Mind, are but *temporary*, and he holds them, but till better evidence repeal his former apprehensions.   He won't defile his assent by prostituting it to every conjecture, or stuff his belief, with the luggage of uncertainties. The modesty of his expression renders him *infallible* ; and while he only saith, he *Thinks so*, he cannot be deceiv'd, or ever assert a *falshood.*   But the wise Monseur *Charron* hath fully discourst of this *Universal liberty*, and sav'd me the labour of enlarging.   Upon the Review of my former considerations, I cannot quarrel with his *Motto* : in a sense *Je ne scay*, is a justifiable *Scepticism*, and not mis-becoming a Candidate of *wisdom.   So-crates* in the judgement of the *Oracle* knew more then *All men*, who in his own knew the least of *any*.

AN APOLOGY FOR
PHILOSOPHY.

AN APOLOGY FOR PHILOSOPHY.

IT is the glory of *Philosophy*, that *Ignorance* and *Phrensie* are it's Enemies ; and it may seem less needful to defend *It* against *stupid* and *Enthusiastick Ignorants*. However, least my discourse should be an advantage in the hands of *phancy* and *folly* ; or, which is the greater mischief, lest it should discourage any of the more enlarged spirits from modest enquiries into Nature ; I'le subjoyn this brief *Apology*.

If *Philosophy* be *uncertain*, the former will confidently conclude it *vain* ; and the later may be in danger of pronouncing the same on their pains, who seek it ; if after all their labour they must reap the wind, meer opinion and conjecture.

But there's a part of Philosophy, that owes no answer to the charge. The *Scepticks'* ΠΑΝΤΑ ΕΣΤΙΝ ΑΟΡΙΣΤΑ, must have the qualification of an exception ; and at least the *Mathematicks* must be priviledg'd

from the endictment.   Neither are we yet at
so deplorable a loss, in the other parts of
what we call *Science* ; but that we may meet
with what will content ingenuity, at this distance from perfection, though all things will
not compleatly satisfie strict and rigid *enquiry*. *Philosophy* indeed cannot immortalize
us, or free us from the inseparable attendants
on this state, *Ignorance*, and *Error*. But
shall we malign it, because it entitles us not
to an *Omniscience*? Is it just to condemn the
Physitian, because *Hephestion* dyed?   Compleat knowledge is reserved to gratifie our
glorified faculties.   We are ignorant of some
things from our *specifical* incapacity; of more
from our *contracted* depravities : and 'tis no
fault in the *spectacles*, that the *blind man* sees
not.   Shall we, like sullen children, because
we have not what we would ; contemn what
the benignty of Heaven offers us ?   Do what
we can, we shall be imperfect in all our
attainments ; and shall we scornfully neglect
what we may reach, because some things are
denyed us?   'Tis madness, to refuse the
Largesses of divine bounty on *Earth*, because
there is not an *Heaven* in them.   Shall we
not rejoyce at the gladsome approach of day,
because it's overcast with a cloud and follow'd

by the obscurity of night? All sublunary
vouchsafements have their allay of a contrary;
and uncertainty, in another kind, is the
annex of all things this side the *Sun*. Even
Crowns and Diadems, the most splendid
parts of terrene attains, are akin to that,
which *to day is in the field*, and *to morrow is
cut down*, and *wither'd*: He that enjoy'd
them, and knew their worth, excepted them
not out of the charge of *Universal Vanity*.
And yet the Politician thinks they deserve
his pains; and is not discourag'd at the
inconstancy of humane affairs, and the
lubricity of his subject.

He that looks for perfection, must seek it
above the *Empyreum*; it is reserv'd for
Glory. It's that alone, which needs not the
advantage of a foyl: Defects seem as
necessary to our now happiness, as their
Opposites. The most refulgent colours are
the result of light and shadows : *Venus* was
never the less beautiful for her Mole. And
'tis for the Majesty of Nature, like the *Per-
sian Kings*, sometimes to cover, and not
alway to prostrate her beauties to the *naked
view* : yea, they contract a kind of splendour
from the seemingly obscuring veil ; which
adds to the enravishments of her transported

admirers. He alone sees all things with an unshadowed comprehensive *Vision*, who eminently is *All* : Only the God of *Nature* perfectly knows her : and light without darkness is the incommunicable claim of him, that dwells in *Light inaccessible*. 'Tis no disparagement to *Philosophy*, that it cannot *Deifie* us, or make good the impossible promise of the *Primitive Deceiver*. It is that, which she owns above her, that must perfectly remake us after the Image of our Maker.

And yet those raised contemplations of God and Nature, wherewith *Philosophy* doth acquaint us ; enlarge and ennoble the spirit, and infinitely advance it above an ordinary level. The soul is alway like the objects of its delight and converse. A *Prince* is as much above a *Peasant* in *spirit*, as *condition* : And Man as far transcends the Beasts in largeness of desire, as dignity of Nature and employment. While we only converse with *Earth*, we are *like* it ; that is, unlike our selves : But when engag'd in more refin'd and intellectual entertainments ; we are somewhat more, then this narrow circumference of flesh speaks us. And, me thinks, those generous *Vertuosi*, who dwell in an higher Region then other Mortals, should make a middle species between the *Platonical* OEOI, and *common Humanity.* Even our Age in variety of glorious exam: ples, can confute the conceit, that *Souls* are *equal*: And the only instance of that *Constellation* of Illustrious Worthies, which compose *The ROYAL SOCIETY*, is enough to strike dead the opinion of the Worlds decay, and conclude it in it's Prime. Reflecting upon which great persons, me thinks I could easily believe, that Men may differ from one another, as much as *Angels* do from *unbodyed Souls.* And perhaps more can be pleaded for such a *Metaphysical Innovation*, then can for a *specifical* diversity among the *Beasts.* Such as these, being in good part freed from the intanglements of *sense* and *body*, are imployed like the spirits above ; in contemplating the divine Artifice and wisdom in the works of Nature ; a kind of anticipation of the *Æthereal* happiness and imployment. This is one part of the *Life* of *Souls.*

While we indulge to the *Sensitive* or *Plantal* Life, our delights are common to us with the creatures *below us*: and 'tis likely, they exceed us as much in them as in

O

the senses their subjects ; and that's a poor happiness for Man to aim at, in which Beasts are his Superiours. But those *Mecurial* spirits which were only lent the Earth to shew Men their folly in admiring it ; possess delights of a nobler make and nature, which as it were antedate *Immortality* ; and at an humble distance, resemble the joyes of the world of *Light* and *Glory*. The *Sun* and *Stars*, are not the worlds *Eyes*, but *These* : The *Celestial Argus* cannot glory in such an universal view. These out-travel theirs, and their *Monarchs* beams : passing into *Vortexes* beyond their Light and Influence ; and with an easie twinkle of an Intellectual Eye look into the *Centre*, which is obscur'd from the upper Luminaries. This is somewhat like the Image of *Omnipresence*: And what the *Hermetical Philosophy* saith of *God*, is in a sense verifiable of the thus *ennobled soul*, That *its Centre is every where, but its circumference no where*. This is the ΑΛΗΘΙΝΟΣ ΑΝΘΡΩΠΟΣ ; and what *Plotinus* calls so, the *divine life*, is somewhat more. Those that live but to the lower *concupiscible*, and relish no delights but *sensual* ; it's by the favour of a *Metaphor*, that we call them *Men.* As *Aristotle* saith of Brutes, they have but the Μιμήματα ἀνθρωπίνης ζωῆς, only some shews and *Apish imitations* of *Humane*; and have little more to justifie their Title to Rationality, then those *Mimick Animals*, the supposed *Posterity* of *Cham*: who, had they retained the priviledge of Speech, which some of the Fathers say they own'd before the *Fall*; it may be they would plead their cause with them, and have laid strong claim to a Parity. Such, as these, are *Philosophie's* Maligners, who computing the usefulness of all things, by what they bring to their *Barns*, and *Treasures*; stick not to pronounce the most generous contemplations, needless unprofitable subtilties: and they might with as good reason say, that the *light* of their Eyes was a superfluous provision of Nature, because it fills not their *Bellies*.

Thus the greatest part of miserable Humanity is lost in *Earth*: and, if Man be an *inversed plant*; these are *inversed Men*; who forgetting that *Sursum*, which Nature writ in their Foreheads, take their Roots in this sordid Element. But the *Philosophical soul* is an *inverted Pyramid*; Earth hath but a point of this *Æthereal cone. Aquila non*

O 2

captat muscas, The Royal Eagle flies not but
at noble Game ; and a young *Alexander* will
not play but with Monarchs. He that hath
been cradled in Majesty, and used to Crowns
and Scepters ; will not leave the Throne to
play with beggars at *Put-pin*, or be fond
of *Tops* and *Cherry-stones* : neither will a
Spirit that dwells with Stars, dabble in this
impurer Mud ; or stoop to be a Play-fellow
and Copartner in delights with the Creatures
that have nought but *Animal*. And though
it be necessitated by its relation to flesh to a
Terrestrial converse ; yet 'tis like the *Sun*,
without contaminating its Beams. For,
though the body by a kind of *Magnetism* be
drawn down to this *Sediment* of universal
dreggs ; yet the thus impregnate spirit contracts a *Verticity* to objects above the *Pole* :
And, like as in a falling Torch, though the
grosser Materials hasten to their Element ;
yet the flame aspires, and, could it master
the dulness of its load, would carry it off from
the stupid Earth it tends to. Thus do those
enobled souls justifie *Aristotles* Νοῦς Θύραθεν
κὰι Θεῖος μόνον ; and in allayed sense that
title, which the Stoicks give it, of ἀπόσπασμα
Θεοῦ. If we say, they are not in their
bodies, but their bodies in them ; we have

the Authority of the divine *Plato* to vouch us : And by the favour of an easie similie we may affirm them to be to the body, as the light of a Candle to the gross, and fæculent snuff; which, as it is not pent up in it, so neither doth it partake of its stench and impurity. Thus, as the *Roman* Orator elegantly descants, *Erigimur, & latiores fieri videmur*; *humana despicimus, contemplantesq*; *supera & cœlestia, hæc nostra, ut exigua, & minima, contemnimus.*

And yet there's an higher degree, to which *Philosophy* sublimes us. For, as it teacheth a generous contempt of what the grovelling desires of *creeping* Mortals Idolize and dote on ; so it raiseth us to love and admire an Object, that is as much above terrestrial as *Infinite* can make it. If *Plutarch* may have credit, the observation of Natures Harmony in the *celestial motions* was one of the first inducements to the belief of *a God* : And a greater then he affirms, that the visible things of the Creation declare him, that made them. What knowledge we have of them we have in a sense of their Authour. His face cannot be beheld by Creature-Opticks, without the allay of a reflexion ; and Nature is one of those mirrors, that represents him to us. And now the more we know of him, the more we love him, the more we are like him, the more we admire him. 'Tis here, that *knowledge wonders*; and there's an *Admiration*, that's not the *Daughter* of *Ignorance*. This indeed stupidly gazeth at the unwonted *effect*: But the Philosophick passion truly admires and adores the supreme *Efficient*. The *wonders* of the Almighty are not seen, but by those that go *down into the deep*. The *Heavens* declare their *Makers Glory*; and *Philosophy theirs*, which by a grateful rebound returns to its *Original source*. The twinkling spangles, the Ornaments of the upper world; lose their beauty and magnificence; while they are but the objects of our narrow'd senses: By them the *half* is not *told us*; and vulgar spectators see them, but as a confused huddle of petty *Illuminants*. But *Philosophy* doth right to those *immense sphears*, and advantagiously represents their Glories, both in the vastness of their *proportions*, and regularity of their *motions*. If we would see the wonders of the *Globe* we dwell in; *Philosophy* must rear us above it. The works of God speak forth his mighty praise: A speech not understood, but by those that *know them*.

The most artful melody receives but little tribute of Honour from the *gazing beasts* ; it requires skill to relish *it.* The most delicate musical accents of the *Indians*, to us are but *inarticulate hummings* ; as questionless are ours to their otherwise *tuned Organs.* Ignorance of the Notes and Proportions, renders all *Harmony* unaffecting. A gay Puppet pleaseth children more, then the exactest piece of *unaffected Art:* it requires some degrees of *Perfection*, to admire what is truly *perfect*, as it's said to be an advance in Oratory to relish *Cicero.* Indeed the unobservant Multitude, may have some general confus'd apprehensions of a kind of *beauty*, that guilds the outside frame of the Universe : But they are Natures courser *wares*, that lye on the *stall*, exposed to the transient view of every *common Eye* ; her choicer *Riches* are lock't up only for the sight of *them*, that will buy at the expence of *sweat* and *Oyl.* Yea, and the visible Creation is far otherwise apprehended by the *Philosophical Inquirer*, then the *unintelligent Vulgar.* Thus the *Physitian* looks with another Eye on the *Medicinal hearb*, then the *grazing Oxe*, which swoops it in with the common *grass* : and the Swine may see the *Pearl*, which yet he values but with the *ordinary muck* ; it's otherwise pris'd by the skilful *Jeweller*.

And from this last Article, I think, I may conclude the charge, which hot-brain'd folly layes in against *Philosophy* ; that it leads to *Irreligion*, frivolous and vain. I dare say, next after the *divine Word*, it's one of the best friends to *Piety*. Neither is it any more justly accountable for the impious irregularities of some, that have paid an homage to its shrine ; then *Religion* it self for the extravagances both *opinionative* and *practick* of high pretenders to it. It is a vulgar conceit, that *Philosophy* holds a confederacy with *Atheism* it self, but most *injurious* : for nothing can better antidote us against it : and they may as well say, that *Physitians* are the only *murtherers*. A *Philosophick Atheist*, is as good sense as a *Divine one* : and I dare say the Proverb, *Ubi tres Medici, duo Athei*, is a Scandal. I think the Original of this conceit might be, That the Students of Nature, conscious to her more *cryptick* wayes of working, resolve many strange effects into the nearer efficiency of *second causes*; which common *Ignorance* and *Superstition* attribute to the Immediate causality of the *first* : thinking it to derogate from the

Divine Power, that any thing which is above their apprehensions, should not be reckon'd above *Natures* activity ; though it be but his Instrument, and works nothing but as impower'd from him.   Hence they violently declaim against all, that will not acknowledge a *Miracle* in every extraordinary effect, as setting Nature in the Throne of *God* ; and so it's an easie step to say, they deny him. When as indeed, Nature is but the chain of second causes ; and to suppose second causes without a first, is beneath the *Logick* of *Gotham.*   Neither can they (who, to make their reproach of Philosophy more *authentick* alledge the Authority of an *Apostle* to conclude it *vain*) upon any whit more reasonable terms make good their charge ; since this allegation stands in force but against its *abuse, corrupt sophistry*, or *traditionary impositions*, which lurk'd under the mask of so serious a name : at the worst, the Text will never warrant an universal conclusion any more ; then that other, where the Apostle speaks of *silly women*, (who yet are the most rigid urgers of this) can justly blot the *sex* with an unexceptionable note of *infamy.*

Now, what I have said here in this short

Apology for *Philosophy*, is not so strictly verifiable of any that I know, as the *Cartesian*. The entertainment of which among truly ingenuous unpossest *Spirits*, renders an after-commendation superfluous and impertinent. It would require a *wit* like its Authors, to do it right in an *Encomium*. The strict Rationality of the *Hypothesis* in the main, and the *critical* coherence of its parts, I doubt not but will bear it down to Posterity with a *Glory*, that shall know no *term*, but the *Universal ruines*. Neither can the *Pedantry*, or prejudice of the present Age, any more obstruct its motion in that *supreme sphear*, wherein its desert hath plac'd it; then can the howling Wolves pluck *Cynthia* from her *Orb* ; who regardless of their noise, securely glides through the undisturbed *Æther*. Censure here will disparage it self, not *it*. He that accuseth the *Sun* of *darkness*, shames his own *blind eyes* ; not its *light*. The barking of *Cynicks* at that *Hero's* Chariot-wheels, will not sully the glory of his *Triumphs*. But I shall supersede this *endless* attempt : *Sun-beams* best commend themselves.

F I N I S .

PRINTED BY
KELLY AND CO., GATE STREET, LINCOLN'S INN FIELDS;
AND KINGSTON-ON-THAMES.

15121666R0

Printed in Great Britain by
Amazon.co.uk, Ltd.,
Marston Gate.